THE ART OF PARENTING WORKBOOK

The Art of Parenting Workbook

PRACTICAL EXERCISES AND ACTIVITIES FOR NURTURING FAMILIES

K.C. DREISBACH, LMFT

Krystal Dreisbach, Licensed Marriage and Family Therapist, Inc

For my Momma, with much love. Thank you for always being a nurturing presence in my life.

Contents

Introduction: Becoming the Best Parent You Can Be!

Welcome to your journey on becoming the best parent that you can be! Wherever you are on your path, congratulations! Parenthood is a rewarding experience filled with moments of pride, joy, and love. I'm going to be honest with you, though, and admit something that most parents don't want to admit to anyone in public:

Parenting (sometimes) just sucks!

Every single parent thinks this at some point in their parenting journey. And they are flat out lying to you if they ever deny it. As a family therapist and a mother of two kids under the age of 8, I can attest to the true horror show that parenting can sometimes be (I once worked with a 16-year-old that caused over $10,000 worth of damage to her family's home!). But does it really have to be that way? Of course not! Although parenting is one of the most challenging gigs around, most parents struggle with it because they have *no clue* what they're doing. They fly from one parental decision to the next with little thought behind the bigger picture of *why* they just made that choice. Every single "Mom Blog," parenting magazine, and parenting book out there is a testament to the hunger that exists for knowledge on the secrets of *how*-to parent.

If you were to search for a parenting book, you'll find thousands of great possibilities, many of which are written by brilliant and exceptional authors, but they all share a similar problem... they're always about the kid! They are all about managing, changing, and manipulating the child into obedience. They all *tell* you *what* to do versus *teach* you *how* to do it.

Here's the problem with that approach: you will know a lot of parenting techniques, but you won't necessarily be a better parent. Think of it this way, does following a recipe make you a chef? Are you suddenly a better cook because you followed the directions in a cookbook? I'm hoping you answered *no*.

If you've done any cooking in your past, you'll know that there's a lot more to being a good cook than just following recipes. There's a certain *art* to it that only experience, skill, and knowledge can provide you. It's through being *taught* the essence of cooking that you truly learn *how* to cook. Essentially, as you learn the *art* of cooking, you *become* a better cook.

And therein lies the problem....

Most of the parenting books you'll find out there today are a recipe. They tell you what ingredients to put into the mix, how long to set the timer, and give you a false impression of what the outcome should look like. (I don't know about you, but my food never looks nearly as pretty or tantalizing as the picture on the recipe.) You might have also noticed that most parenting books are very specific on who they are meant for. You'll find parenting books on parenting babies, parenting toddlers, parenting teenagers, parenting oppositional children, parenting stubborn children, parenting boys, parenting girls, and so on. The list is endless!

Did you ever wonder why this is? Why are all parenting books *so* specific? It's because they are like that cooking recipe. You can't find a dessert recipe that also gives you a chicken dinner. Recipes are very specific because they are intended to produce a very specific outcome. They aren't there to *teach* you *how* to cook. They're there to *tell* you *what* to do so you produce a meal.

But what if there was a different way?

What if you could find a parenting book that actually *taught* you *how* to parent? A book that *taught* you the skills behind parenting so that you could parent your child regardless of whether they were a toddler, a teenager, a boy, a girl, and so on? A book that *taught* you the *art* of parenting?

You just might have found that book....

This book, along with its companion, is going to lay down the groundwork and foundation for successful parenting throughout your child's lifespan. It is purposefully written to be adaptable to children of any age, gender, or temperament, making this text unique in its approach as a parenting book. I take a wholistic approach to parenting that focuses on the emotional growth and empowerment of the parent versus solely dissecting the child and listing out disciplinary tools.

My goal is to grow *you*, as a parent, so that you can learn the fine art that is parenting. I want *you* to become more knowledgeable about your child's development, to develop the skills you need to create a healthy and positive family environment, and to guide *you* on a journey of self-discovery. Through this process of self-growth, you will not only learn to raise happier and emotionally-healthier children, but you will also grow and develop a deeper, more meaningful sense of purpose as you learn the fine art of parenting. Essentially, parents will be taught *how* to become a *better* parent for a lifetime of family joy and fulfillment.

But why should you trust me?

It can be hard to trust someone you've never met before and know nothing about. Let me help ease some of your hesitations. As mentioned previously, I am a licensed Marriage and Family therapist, specializing in parenting and working with troubled youth. Over the course of my career, not only have I successfully treated and worked with thousands of children and families in family therapy, I've also taught parenting classes to low-income families, have lectured to graduate students for the past 3 years on topics involving the care and parenting of foster youth, and have provided seminars to various school districts on the psycho-social development of youth to help teachers better understand their students. For years I've served as a Clinical Supervisor in non-profit agencies to help teach and develop new mental health therapists and ensure the quality of care they provide to families. Furthermore, for the past several years, I've shared my parenting expertise through freelance writing as a guest blogger for various popular parenting blogs, and I write regular articles on various parenting topics through my own website.

Most importantly, I am a real mom of two kids, living the day-to-day struggles that every modern parent is dealing with. In my work with families, it is my genuineness and honesty, combined with my clinical knowledge and expertise, that has allowed me to reach and work so effectively with families of varying backgrounds.

As a professional in the field of working with parents and their children, I have seen firsthand the need for a book that is about the *growth* of the parent versus the *raising* of the child. *This* is The *Art of Parenting* series. This unique approach allows me to help you create a loving and structured foundation for your family that you can use no matter how old your child is or what difficulties your child may be facing. This approach will effectively bridge the gap between *telling* you *what* to do and *teaching* you *how* to do it. Get ready to grow as a parent and effectively learn the **Art of Parenting.**

So why create the workbook edition?

If you are using this workbook, the hope is that you have read the companion book, *The Art of Parenting: How to Parent from Infancy to Adulthood* (*AoP*). The workbook is intended as a supplement to the main text, giving you more information, ideas, reflection questions, and exercises to try. Each chapter will contain a "diet" version of the information contained in the original book.

If you haven't read *AoP*, you should be able to limp along with the information in each chapter. I caution you, however, that some of the concepts discussed are complex, and you might still find yourself confused without the full-length book. *AoP* provided much detail, real-life case examples, definitions, and more to help you understand each concept as best as possible. This workbook edition will be more focused on providing the basic information needed for each concept and the corresponding exercises for each chapter. Case examples, definitions, and some of the other material provided in the main text have been removed to help "lean" this book out.

So, let's chat a little more about what you will find in the workbook addition. As a Clinical Supervisor, I found that many of the clinicians that worked under my license struggled with helping parents. They would focus *only* on the child, only to discover that there would be little improvement OR that the child would improve, discharge from therapy, and then be back at our door several months (sometimes a year) later. Why is this?

It quickly became obvious that the families were struggling to sustain the improvements they had made in the therapy room. Several factors came into play as to why this would happen (remember the Wholistic Parenting Map!), but at its core, the therapists failed to do sufficient work with the parent.

It's important to note that when I say there wasn't sufficient work done with the parent, I am in no way "blaming" the parent. Instead, what I am suggesting is that there wasn't enough *support* given to the parent to help them learn how to manage their specific child. In *AoP*, we spoke significantly about how important the parent is in the Parent-Child relationship. Giving therapy only to the child is like bathing a dog to get rid of fleas without treating the dog with a flea prevention solution. The fleas will just come right back. The bath only provides temporary relief.

Unfortunately, many therapists are underprepared to adequately work with families and parents. It doesn't matter what discipline you look at: psychology, social work, marriage and family therapy, etc. There is so much a therapist needs to learn during their graduate studies, that only the basics are given to them. As such, they fail to focus on one of the most valuable pieces of the family system: the parent.

All of this is to give you some understanding about why it was so important to create a workbook. After writing *AoP*, I was reminded that, the best way to learn anything is by *doing*. *AoP* gave you the information, but did you really embody it? Did it sink into your psyche and start to change

the way you live your day-to-day parenting life? Maybe... Maybe not....
Rarely do we learn anything new by simply reading about it. We need action! We need to reflect, to question, to practice, to *do* something with it!
That's what this edition is all about, taking you to the next level of understanding.

How should you use this workbook?

As you go through each chapter, you'll be given a mini refresher on the topic. After that, you'll find an assortment of exercises to help you grow and become the best parent you can be. Here are the types of exercises you can expect:

- **Reflect**- These exercises are questions designed to help you consider things you might not have thought of before. Their main purpose is to help you develop insight into your own parenting practices. They will be accompanied by space to jot down notes and any thoughts you had that strike you as important.
- **Connect**- Connect exercises are designed to help you make the connection between the material in this book and your own parenting. They are here to help you bridge the gap between text material and real life, hopefully giving you some "light bulb" moments.
- **Respond**- These exercises involve action. This is where you will put yourself to work and truly begin applying what you've learned from this book. Expect to have discussions with your family, trying new parenting techniques, and really exercising those parenting muscles!

Not every chapter of the book will have all 3 types of exercises, but you should see at least 1 for every chapter. To make the most use of this book, take the time to really reflect, write, and practice. Remember, no one ever learned anything from just reading about it. You must *do* something!

With that said, let me mention just a few more things before we begin. I do try to keep gender in mind as I write, referring to gender-neutral terms, such as "parent" throughout the book. To keep the flow of writing, and to avoid overuse of these gender-neutral terms, please realize that I may refer to terms like *mother, father, dad, etc.* Recognize that this is not done to only reference one gender, but rather, to keep the writing of this book from being bogged down. At any time that I say "dad," it could (and should) be easily switched in your mind to "mom" and vice versa. Furthermore, I will utilize male pronouns (he, his, him) and plural pronouns (they, them, their) throughout the book as opposed to saying "he/she," "him/her," etc. Once again, this is simply to ease the flow of writing. At any point, feel free to change the pronouns in your mind as you read. In this way, these stories and techniques better reflect you and your current parenting situation. I wish you much luck on your parenting journey. Now get ready to dig in and get to work!

Are *you* ready?

1

Wholistic Parenting

I've been a therapist for a long time, and for the length of my entire career, my focus has been on working with families. When I became a mother myself, I applied what I had learned as a therapist to my role as a parent. Essentially, I was making sure that I was "walking the walk" and not just "talking the talk." That was extremely important to me. Not only because I wanted to make sure my children were successful or because I knew that these techniques worked, but because I firmly believed that whatever I asked of my clients, I had to be willing to do myself.

In *AoP*, we delved deep into Wholistic Parenting, my system for understanding all the factors that affect, contribute to, and make up your parenting. The analogy we used was "spinning plates." Each plate is a component to the parenting job that you must keep in mind, but you must keep every single plate in mind 100% of the time. If you don't, that's how you accidentally drop one. And when one falls, another one is likely to drop too. That's parenting in a nutshell!

When you become a Wholistic Parent, you become knowledgeable of each one of those spinning plates. Since you have this knowledge, you can seek out and acquire parenting techniques that make sense for you and your family. You can adapt different techniques to make them fit your parenting needs, and you are able to take life's curve balls with more grace and calm. This is the value of taking a Wholistic Parenting approach.

Today, we're going to review Wholistic Parenting by mapping out all the pieces that comprise of the mind, body, and environment for you and your family. I'll help you to see each of those spinning plates, so you have a greater awareness of what being a parent is *really* all about.

1.1 Reviewing Wholistic Parenting

I would be lying if I were to say that Wholistic Parenting is easy- it isn't. There are so many parts that it can feel a little overwhelming. To help us better capture what Wholistic Parenting is all about, I created a map to reference as we break down all the layers. Look at this map now. You can find it at the back of the book in Appendix A.

It's a lot, right? You probably don't even know what you are looking at, and who could blame you? When I broke it all down myself, I went through many iterations of it. Eventually, I landed on this. I'm willing to accept that it's not perfect by any means, but I think it's the closest thing out there to truly mapping out all the pieces that go into parenting. Thus, this is a picture of Wholistic Parenting. Now that we have an idea of what this encompasses, let's take a closer look and break it down.

The 3 Main Branches

To begin, we'll start by looking at those 3 main branches. Those are the 3 main components that everything else will stem from. They are:

1. **Familial Environment**- This is your home and the multiple parts that go with it.

2. **Social Environment**- This is the outside world that your family lives in. It consists of your neighborhood, social networks, country, and current events.
3. **Child**- This is your child and the unique parts about them that you'll need to keep in mind as you work to parent this person.

These are the big heavy hitters, and when you are parenting, these are the 3 big pieces that are going to affect you and your effectiveness as a parent. You'll need to keep these 3 spinning plates in mind to do this job to the best of your ability.

Familial Environment

When we look at the Familial Environment, we can see that it is further broken down into an additional 3 parts. They consist of:

- Parent
- Discipline
- Family Narrative

Hopefully, it makes sense that the family environment would be further broken down into these pieces. Each one of these components are broken down further into more detail. The first one is **Parent**. There are many factors that will affect your parenting, including your:

- Physical Health
- Emotional/Mental Health
- Spiritual Health (if applicable to you)
- Knowledge about Parenting
- Skill Set (related to parenting)
- Time (or lack thereof)

These are all layers that affect you as a person. Anything that affects you, is going to affect your family. As such, it's a BIG part of the Familial Environment.

Next is **Discipline**. This one doesn't have as many pieces, but it's still an incredibly important factor to effective parenting. The 3 components that make up Discipline include:

- Rules & Healthy Boundaries
- Structure & Routine
- Rewards & Consequences

These 3 parts are very much interwoven. They must be considered individually but executed as a solid unit. Trust me, that's incredibly hard to do! But it's possible. All it takes is practice. We will be digging deep into discipline in chapter 9.

Finally, you have the **Family Narrative**. This is a big concept but, essentially, it's your family's story. I'll explain it further in chapter 5 and again in chapter 11.

The Family Narrative is further broken down into 2 parts that consist of:

- Ethnic Culture
- Parent-Child Relationship

Your **Ethnic Culture** is going to be a part of your family's story and is, essentially, your family's ethnicity. It impacts everything about you, from how you dress and speak, to the foods you eat, and even how you interact with others.

Your **Parent-Child Relationship** is essentially the bond you have with your child. I further broke down this concept into 3 more factors:

- Healthy Boundaries
- Quality Time

- Warmth, Love, & Attunement

In chapter 3, we will dive into the Parent-Child relationship with much more depth. Then, in chapter 5, you'll learn more about the parent-child relationship and quality time.

Social Environment

When we look at the **Social Environment**, we can see there are 3 parts to it. It consists of:

- Social Culture
- Current Events
- Social Influence

Social Culture is similar to ethnic culture, but also different. Let's say you are Cuban, and this is your Ethnic Culture. If you live in Cuba, it will also be your Social Culture. If you live in the United States, however, this is no longer your Social Culture. Your Social Culture now becomes that of the area in which you live. As such, your Social Culture is subject to change depending on where your family currently resides.

Current Events greatly impact your parenting, whether you like it or not. If you live in an active war zone, that will cause you to be more protective, fearful, and anxious. This will certainly change what you allow your children to do daily. This is an extreme example, but it effectively demonstrates how current events will contribute to your parenting. Over examples might be government elections, pandemics, natural disasters, or civil unrest.

Social Influence consists of the people that might influence you or your child. Right now, I might be a social influence on you, which might cause a shift in how you parent. Your child's peers are a social influence on them, which may cause them to behave in ways you approve or disapprove of. Other social influences include neighbors, the media, and extended family among other things.

The Child

Hopefully, it makes sense that your child would be further broken down into multiple parts, just like you were as the parent. Those pieces include your child's:

- Physical Health
- Emotional/Mental Health
- Spiritual Health (if applicable to them)
- Developmental Age
- Sibling Position

These are all layers that affect your child as a person. And anything that affects your child, is going to affect how he behaves, which will then affect how you respond to him. As such, it's a BIG part of Wholistic Parenting.

Remember, Wholistic Parenting is the key to successful parenting and a happy, loving, and untied family. It's time to evolve into the best parent that you can be. Let's begin....

1.2 Exercises

It's time to roll up our sleeves and get to work! This book's focus will be, primarily, on the parts of Wholistic Parenting that you can actually control. That's the *Familial Environment* (i.e. Parent, Discipline, and Family Narrative) and some parts of the *Child*. But it's important to remember that there is 1 other main branch (*Social Environment*) that is important and will impact your parenting. Although we won't be exploring this branch in the rest of this book, I thought it would be a good idea to spend some time with it before we move on. As such, let's look at each part of this branch: Social Culture, Current Events, and Social Influence.

Social Environment: Social Culture

To begin, have you ever taken time to think about your Social Culture? Remember, Social Culture is defined as the related characteristics, spiritual beliefs, languages, customs, and cultural heritage of the society in which your family lives. The culture where you live will impact you. It might impact the language you speak, the foods you eat, the holidays you celebrate, and it might even impact your parenting.

Exercise: Reflect

I'm going to pose a series of questions. In order to reap the full benefit of this workbook, take a moment to genuinely reflect on each question. If it doesn't apply to you, then move on to the next one. If it does apply to you, I recommend taking note of your answers and jotting them down. Remember to be honest with yourself. This book is for you! No one else has to know the answers.

Take a moment to reflect on the following questions and write your thoughts on the lines provided:

- Religion/Spirituality
    - Does your family have a religion or spirituality you follow? If so, what is it?
    - How does this spirituality and/or religious community affect your parenting? What guidance does it provide?
    - Does your surrounding community and/or neighborhood adhere to a specific religious and/or spiritual belief? Is it the same or different than your own?

Does it help you feel supported as a parent or alienated?

_____

_____

_____

_____

_____

_____

- Neighborhood/Community
    - What is the community like where you live? Do you feel safe? Do you feel your children are safe?
    - Do you allow your children to walk to school alone in the mornings? Do you allow them to go for walks by themselves in your neighborhood?
    - Would you define your neighborhood as "peaceful," "dangerous," or "conflictual"? How does this definition impact your daily life? How does it impact your parenting?
    - What language do you speak? How about your children? Do they speak the same language as you? What language does your community speak? Do you find yourself needing to rely on your children as interpreters to accomplish simple tasks? How does this impact your parenting?

_____

_____

_____

_____

_____

_____

- Local Customs
    - ◦ Does your community celebrate any specific holidays? Is this a holiday you've always celebrated yourself?
    - ◦ Why do you celebrate these holidays? Do they matter to you or do you do it because "everyone else is doing it"?
    - ◦ How do these holidays affect your family? Consider the traditions you might share as a family because of these holidays. Does your community celebrate a holiday that your family does not? If so, do you find yourself arguing or frequently explaining to your kids why your family doesn't celebrate the same holidays as your community?
    - ◦ Does your family dress differently from others in your community? How does this impact your children? Is this a topic that you find yourself constantly arguing with your children about?

_____

_____

_____

_____

_____

_____

_____

Exercise: Connect

Now that you've taken some time to reflect and jot down some notes, let's take a look at it all together. Review your responses now. What do you notice? What parts of your Social Culture are currently impacting you, your family, and your parenting? Write them down:

_____

_____

_____

_____

_____

_____

Most likely, you probably determined that some aspects of your Social Culture are directly impacting you. Maybe you live in an unsavory neighborhood leading you to shelter your children more out of fear. Or, perhaps you practice a religion that isn't practiced by the majority of the people in your community. As such, you might find yourself frequently arguing with your children about why you don't practice the same customs as their friends.

Can you see how these outside factors, your Social Culture, impacts your parenting? The impact might be small or it could be huge, but it's playing a role in one way or another. It's important for you to recognize that. Your family is not being raised in a vacuum, and that means that the sooner you can connect how your Social Culture is impacting your children and parenting, the sooner you can begin to respond in a thoughtful way.

Exercise: Respond

Not only are these factors impacting your parenting, but they are impacting your kids. Have you ever taken a moment to think about how these factors affect them? Maybe you have. If you haven't, here's your chance!

If you have an older child, now's the time to begin a dialogue with them about the impacts of Social Culture. Find an opportunity free of distractions. Perhaps go out to lunch together or go for a walk. I want you to look back at the Connect Exercise and make a mental note about the items you identified. Then, I want you to ask your child how these items impact them. Consider some of the following questions:

- How does this affect you?
- Do you ever feel angry with me because of this? If so, why?
- Do you ever feel sad about this? If so, why?
- What's it like for you to experience this?
- Does anyone bully you at school because of this?
- Do you keep this part of yourself a secret? If so, why?
- How does all of this make you feel?
- Do you understand why our family does this? If yes, can you explain to me what your understanding is?

Without me knowing what your specific factors are, it's difficult for me to tailor these questions specifically to your situation. To help you see these in action, however, let me provide you a sample dialogue of what this might look like with your child.

Example 1:

Renae and her daughter Julie are Jewish, but they are living in a community that is predominately Christian. Renae is taking the time to understand how this factor is affecting Julie.

Renae: Julie, I know we're Jewish and that most of your friends are Christian. Does this ever affect you?

Julie: Nah, not really I guess.

Renae: What about Hanukkah and Christmas? Does it ever bother you then?

Julie: Well, I guess I just don't understand what the big deal is with getting a Christmas tree. Everyone else gets one and my friends always talk about it.

Renae: What's that like for you? How does it make you feel?

Julie: I guess I feel left out. They're always talk about going out with their families to buy Christmas trees. And then they're always talking about presents and stockings and all this other stuff, and I can't really join in on what they're talking about. So, I just feel left out.

Renae: That must be hard. I remember I felt like that when I was a kid too.

Julie: You did?

Renae: Yup. Everyone was always talking about Christmas and Easter, but I couldn't join in the excitement with them. It was hard for me. So I can understand how it must be difficult for you too.

Julie: Yah, it kind of sucks sometimes.

Renae: I know. I understand how you feel. Does anyone ever bully you at school because you don't celebrate Christmas?

Julie: Not really. One time this one kid made fun of me because I didn't know what everyone was talking about. He called me stupid. But normally people leave me alone about it. But sometimes I feel like I'm weird because I celebrate Hanukkah and no one knows what that is. *Everyone* knows about Christmas, but *no one* knows about Hanukkah!

Hopefully, you can see how the conversation with your own child should play out through this example. Take careful notice how Renae never discourages Julie from feeling left out or feeling "weird." Renae also doesn't get upset about this, defensive, or protective. Instead, Renae's mission in this exercise is to explore her daughter's thoughts and emotions about this topic. Renae wants to have a better understanding of what her daughter's experience is and allow Julie to have an open and safe environment to discuss these topics with her. This is invaluable! The more your child feels like they can talk to you openly without you reacting defensively, emotionally, or even protectively, the more they will open up to you honestly.

Now, this doesn't mean that you don't react if your child is being significantly bullied or harmed by someone. Of course you'll need to act! But in this moment, when you are reflecting with your child and trying to understand their experience, it's important that you remain cool, calm, and collect. Ask exploratory questions. This exercise is about discovery and understanding; it's not an interrogation!

Finally, note that Renae and Julie are truly having a dialogue. The conversation is following back and forth between mother and daughter. Renae isn't doing all the talking, and she isn't trying to convince Julie that she should feel differently. By giving Julie the space to express herself without Renae trying to persuade her to feel differently (i.e. *"Don't feel weird. There is nothing weird about you"*), Julie is more likely to communicate openly. This is important. When you try to convince your children to feel differently, you send the unspoken message that their feelings aren't valid. And when children don't feel validated, they begin to close up and bottle up their emotions. As parents, we don't want our children to feel negative emotions or have self-deprecating thoughts, but telling them that they shouldn't think or feel this way doesn't solve the problem. It only creates a bigger one.

Now, let's say you have a younger child who isn't capable yet of having this type of discussion. This exercise will look a little different for you. Instead, I want you to reflect back on your own childhood. Can you remember what Social Cultural factors affected you? What were they? What was the impact like for you? Look at the questions on page 18 and imagine what it would have been like for you if your parent had this dialogue with you. What would the experience look and feel like?

Hopefully, you tried this exercise out. What was it like? What did you learn about your child that you didn't know before? If you reflected back on your own childhood experience, what did you notice?

Take a moment to write down any important insights you had:

_____

_____

_____

_____

_____

Social Environment: Current Events

Whether we like it or not, Current Events in our communities, and sometimes globally, will impact your parenting. In 2020, the world experienced a global pandemic, COVID-19. This was a current event that largely shaped how parents worked with their children. I had clients who wouldn't let their children walk out the front door for fear that their children would get sick.

Exercise: Reflect

Let's take a second to think about how the current events in your community are affecting you right now. Consider the following questions:

- What is happening right now in my community/neighborhood? Consider things such as mass shootings, illnesses, fires, burglaries, wild animal sightings in the area, etc.
- If you can't think of any current events, consider a past one, such as the killing of George Floyd in the United States or the COVID-19 pandemic.
- How has this current event impacted your parenting?
- Do you find yourself reacting differently to situations involving your children or family?
- Have rules in your home changed, such as curfews, bedtimes, or other family routines?

_____

_____

_____

_____

_____

_____

_____

_____

Social Environment: Social Influence

This is a BIG one that impacts families. Friends, extended family members, grandparents, and even teachers or daycare workers can have an impact on you and your kids. One of my favorite examples of this is when my daughter would visit her grandmother's house when she was a toddler. In my home, we had a rule of "no jumping on the sofa." But at her grandmother's house, she was allowed to jump on the furniture to her heart's content. The result? Well, every time she came home from grandma's house, she would begin jumping on all the furniture. It would take me a good day of working with her to get her to stop. As she got older, she would remember that this was a rule I had put in place with her. But, if she was at grandma's house with her cousins (who LOVED jumping on the sofa), then you better believe she would start jumping on the furniture right with them! This is an example of Social Influence.

Exercise: Connect

Have you ever taken the time to think about how the people around you influence your kids? I'm sure you've noticed it before, but maybe you've never really taken the time to comprehend the full impact this might have on you and your child.

For this exercise, I want you to pick one individual that your child visits often. It can be a neighborhood friend, a grandparent, a cousin, aunt or uncle, etc. Pick one for this exercise. Write down who that person is:

_____

_____

_____

Now, take a second to think back on the last time your child visited this person. Did your child act any differently during or after the visit? Here are some examples of behaviors to consider:

- Trying new foods (i.e. toddlers will often try a new food when they see other kids trying it)
- Responding to you in an uncharacteristic way
- Disobeying rules they normally obey
- Dressing differently
- Calling you something different (maybe calling you by your first name or calling you "mom" when normally it's "mommy")
- Regressing to old behaviors, such as whining like a baby when a baby is around
- Listening to music they've never listened to before (common with adolescent kids)
- Suddenly interested in a new activity

Write down what you notice:

_____

_____

_____

_____

_____

_____

Do you see how the people around you influence your child? This, in turn, will impact your parenting. Feel free to repeat this exercise as much as you want. Take a good look at how your social circle (that includes family) and take time to understand how the individuals in this circle act as a positive, negative, or neutral influence on your child AND you!

Exercise: Respond

Now that you've taken the opportunity to assess your Social Influence, let's take this a step further. Have you been able to identify anyone (this includes immediate family members) that is a negative influence on you or your children? Who are those individuals?

_____

_____

_____

_____

_____

_____

Now here comes the hard part... is the negative influence significant enough or harmful enough that eliminating these individuals from your life is something you should consider? This is a hard question, so take a moment to reflect on this.

The reality is, you *want* to keep people around who are a positive influence in your life and the lives of your children. People who are neutral don't make a difference either way, so keeping them around is fine too. But people who negatively impact your family are probably better off gone. The issues arise when you can't cut those individuals out for one reason or another.

Let's slow it all down and look at the individuals you identified as negative influences. Are these people neighbors, friends, teachers, or family members, etc.? If they are people you can cut out easily with no problems, then the problem is solved. But what if you can't?

I had a client once who was a 10-year-old boy with a 3-year-old sister. Unfortunately, the boy had been sexually abused in his past, which led to another problem... he began sexually abusing his 3-year-old sister. I think we can all agree that the brother was a "negative influence" on his little sister, but the mother couldn't just cut her young son out of her life. He was also her child, and he had also been hurt deeply, causing his behavior disturbances. How do you handle situations such as these?

When you can't cut an individual out of your life, the next step is to start instituting healthy boundaries (we'll talk more about this in chapter 2). This might mean instituting new rules, increasing parental supervision, and/or having difficult discussions with these individuals to establish a mutual understanding of the situation.

Go back to your list of individuals that you identified as negative influences and pick one. Now, I want you to determine which one of these interventions you are willing to try:

- Establishing a new rule and corresponding consequence
- Increasing parental supervision
- Engage in a discussion

Write down which one you would like to try:

_____

_____

_____

_____

_____

_____

If you have chosen to establish a new rule and consequence, what will this new rule be? (If you need help with this one, check out chapter 9). If you are going to increase parental supervision, what will that look like? And finally, if you are going to have a discussion, who is that conversation going to be with and what are the talking points you want to have?

Write down your chosen intervention here:

_____

_____

_____

_____

_____

To help you visualize this better, let's look at an example and break it down with each intervention.

Example:

Miranda has identified that her son, Jason, has a neighborhood friend that is a bad influence. Every time the boys are together, her son always picks up bad habits. Most recently, he has been cursing when he plays video games. She has identified that she will need to intervene in order to keep this from becoming a larger issue later on. To tackle this issue, Miranda has established a new rule and corresponding consequence:

- **Rule:** No cursing

- **Consequence:** Cursing leads to losing 15 minutes of video game time

Miranda sits down and talks to Jason about the new rule and consequence. She explains why the behavior is a problem and what words he is allowed to use instead when he is playing video games (i.e. instead of "damn it" he is allowed to use "darn it" or "dang it").

Next, Miranda decides that she will also increase parental supervision. As such, Jason can no longer go to his friend's house, but his friend is welcome to come to her home where she is able to monitor the boys' interactions. She also relocates the video game system downstairs in the family room where she can easily monitor the boys while they play video games together. When Jason's friend comes over, she reminds the boys that cursing is not acceptable. She also warns them that if they curse, she will remove 15 minutes from their video game time.

Finally, Miranda decides that she is going to have a discussion with the other child's mother, Lisa. She finds a day to go over and asks her if she has ever noticed the boys cursing while playing video games. Lisa acknowledges this but shares that it isn't a problem for them in her family. Miranda respects Lisa's opinions. She shares that, when the boys are at her house, she will be reminding them both not to curse. Although Lisa doesn't share Miranda's concern about cursing, she acknowledges that it's Miranda's house, and Miranda sets the rules.

In this example, Miranda utilizes all 3 interventions so that you can see how each intervention might be implemented. You don't have to use all 3 interventions for yourself, but if the situation is severe enough, my recommendation would be to implement as many interventions as you can.

2

Developing Your
Parenting Philosophy

In this chapter, we're going to take a look at parenting philosophies. Specifically, we're going to examine *your* parenting philosophy, and if you don't have one, you'll start developing your own!

2.1 Why have a Parenting Philosophy?

I told you in the last chapter that this book would discuss the fundamentals to parenting so that you could take what I teach you and apply it to the raising of your child, regardless of age, gender, etc. As such, my goal is to help you become a better parent by helping you grow and evolve. Everything needs a solid foundation to be built from. Trees require a strong and dense root structure that keep the tree held high and strong against winds. A house needs a solid foundation to be built upon, or the whole building collapses. Parenting is no different.

Having a parenting philosophy *is* that foundation. It's your fundamental beliefs, concepts, and attitudes that you will use to *root* your future parenting decisions. In many ways, it's the core that you will be able to go back to and rely on when you find yourself unsure of how to proceed in any given parenting dilemma with your child. It will be your compass on your journey.

My Parenting Philosophy- The 7 Key Principles

I'm going to share with you the basic points of my own parenting philosophy, which will create the foundation for our journey together. Then, we will work toward helping you develop your own Parenting Philosophy. As we go through each point, reflect on it. If it feels right to you, then feel free to incorporate it as part of your own parenting foundation. If something doesn't feel right, then don't feel pressured to take it. All I ask is that you take the time to consider *why* that point doesn't feel right to you, and then ask that you adapt it to what's best for you and your family.

1. All Parents are Trying Their Very Best

With some exceptions, I believe that parents generally want what is best for their kids. We are biologically wired to want to raise children who are happy, healthy, and well-adjusted. Unfortunately, other things might come in the way of this, such as substance abuse, traumatic past experiences of abuse or neglect, poor modeling from our own parents, mental health issues, or societal pressures and norms that can come to affect how we parent our children. This, in turn, can cause us to make choices that end up harming our own kids.

2. Parenting is a 24/7 Job

Parenting is a job, a responsibility, and it is seldom easy. It is a difficult task to undertake the caring and raising of a young human being, and it is a task that should be taken seriously. Although being a parent brings with it a wealth of love, laughter, and joyous moments, it is definitely not for the faint of heart. It is a 24 hours, 7 days a week kind of job, with no end in sight. Once a parent, you're always a parent.

3. Your Children Always Come First

Most folks can buy-in to my first two points, but this one becomes a little harder to swallow. Your children should always come first. No matter how tired you are, how hungry or thirsty, or how sick you feel... your child always comes first. Now, as much as I believe that your children should truly come first, I also believe that you must work to find balance. All parents need to take care of themselves too! The reality is, if you physically, mentally, or emotionally fall apart, you will not be able to care for your children. Because of this, your own self-care is vital to the care of your kids! Balance is key to this foundational point. You must place the needs of your children before your own, but within reason, and not at the risk of losing your own sanity.

4. There is No Such Thing as a "Bad" Kid

Evil, "bad" children just don't exist. You *must* believe that your child is inherently *good,* or at the very least *neutral.* Children who do "bad things" are *not* bad children. There are many reasons why a child may engage in rotten behavior, but none of these reasons stem from the child being simply a "bad seed." If you truly believe you simply birthed a "bad apple," then you will also need to accept that there is *nothing* you can do to change it, and you have *zero* control over the situation. If you believe, instead, that your child is inherently "good" (or at the very least "neutral"), then you believe that their *behavior* is "bad," not him or her. If you believe their *behavior* is bad, then I will tell you that *behavior* can be changed.

5. As a Parent, Your Primary Role is to be Your Child's Teacher, Not Their Friend

As a parent, your primary role in your child's life is to be their first and most prominent teacher, not their friend. From the very beginning of that child's life, you will be teaching them everything they need to know about living a successful life as a productive citizen of your culture and society. From morality and ethical standards, to basic social customs, to how to clean their rooms, your lessons will be the most deeply ingrained teachings in their conscious and subconscious minds. And the most important medium you will use to impart these lessons is the Parent-Child Relationship. Always remember, you are the parent; the neighbor kid is their friend.

6. YOU Are the Parent, and Thus, YOU Set the Rules

When we treat our children like our friends, we give them more authority by elevating them into a place of parental power. This is a mistake. Always remember that YOU are the parent and YOU set the rules. Now, in a two-parent household, it is critical that parents approach decision making as a team. One parent should avoid making parental decisions (especially BIG ones) without involving the other parent. Failure to include the second parent in decision making can create a problematic dynamic known as "triangulation." To help us understand this phenomenon a little better, notice the below graphic. This Parent-Child Relational Triangle depicts the parental relationship with the child in the appropriate way:

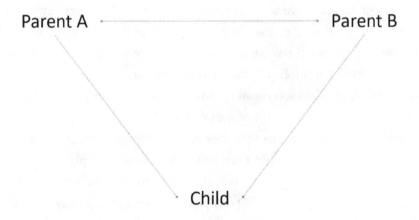

In this graphic, both parents are placed at the top, with equal authority. Rules of the home and parenting are done together, with open communication between both parents. This is depicted by the double-sided arrow. The authority of both of these parents flow downward toward the child in an equal way. Both parents have equal authority over the raising, praising, and disciplining of the child.

Alternatively, in a situation where the child has been elevated to a place of parental authority, our Parent-Child Relational Triangle looks more like this:

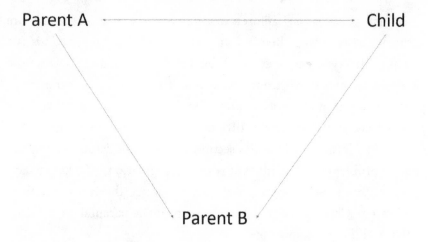

In this diagram, we see that Parent A and the Child share authority with one another (i.e. the double-sided arrow) while the "parental power" for Parent B has been removed (i.e. both arrows point downward toward Parent B). This, in turn, renders Parent B's authority null-and-void. This sets up an erroneous power dynamic in the household. It's a simple enough concept to understand, but most parents would adamantly disagree that they've ever engaged in this second relational pattern. You might even be thinking that right now.

In truth, we all engage in this type of pattern from time to time. This occasional slip is not a big deal, but the more your family slips into this pattern, the more common it becomes. Then, in some families, this ends up becoming the "norm" in the Parent-Child Relationship. Regardless of what the situation is for your family, always remember that *authority* must flow from the parents down to the child. With that said, however, this is not a dictatorship! Don't be a parental tyrant!

7. The Core of the Parent-Child Relationship MUST be in Respect

Your child must respect you and YOU must respect your child. When working with families, I've met with folks who mistakenly think of *respect* and *parental authority* as interchangeable concepts. As such they end up treating their children without respect. From the first day of your child's life, you should treat that baby with respect. Respect needs to be at the core of your relationship with your child. This, in turn, will help create a dynamic where your child respects you too.

Respect should be the cornerstone of your household. Both parents and all children in the home should demonstrate respect to one another. *Respect* and *authority* are not interchangeable concepts, but they are also not mutually exclusive of one another. They frequently go hand-in-hand. The key to remember is that you do not need to have "authority" in any given situation in order to demand "respect." Think of it this way, if you are an employee, you deserve respect, right? Your supervisor can treat you with respect and dignity, regardless of the fact that authority flows down from them to you. The same can be achieved in your household.

Now, in this same vein, let's talk about respect toward your co-parent. Remember how I stated that parents will *accidentally* raise their child to a place of parental authority, and thus, lower the second parent's (i.e. Parent B) parental authority? One of the ways that this easily occurs in families, without anyone really even realizing it, is by treating your co-parent in a way that shows disrespect to that parent. Perhaps you yell at them in front of the children, or say something smug, such as, "You never remember anything," or maybe you even call them a name (i.e. "You're such an idiot"). All of these interactions demonstrate disrespect to your parenting partner. When this is done in front of your child, it sends an unspoken message to your child that you and your co-parent do not share equal parental authority, and this can create all kinds of problems.

2.2 Where Do You Go from Here?

Exercise: Reflect

Have you ever taken the time to consider your own parenting philosophy? We all have one that we parent from instinctually, but few of us ever take the time to really distill what that philosophy is. Take a moment now to reflect on the 7 principles I shared with you. Do you like any of them? If so, which ones?

_____

_____

_____

_____

Are there any that you don't like? If so, which ones are you opposed to?

_____

_____

_____

_____

Remember, it's ok if you don't agree with any or all of the principles I shared. But, if you don't like them, why not? Take a second to reflect on why you don't like that principle? What part about it bothers you?

_____

_____

_____

_____

Exercise: Respond

Now, here's where the tough part comes in. What is your parenting philosophy? There is no set number of principles you should have, but I would encourage you to try and come up with at least 5. Start off by incorporating any of the principles you like from my own parenting philosophy, then add any additional principles that are important to you.

If you have a co-parent, have a discussion with them about their own parenting philosophy. Consider some of the following questions:

- How does their philosophy differ from yours?
- Which principles can you agree on?
- Which ones do you need to compromise on?
- Do any of your principles contradict with theirs?

Remember that, as you grow and evolve as a parent, you might find your principles change a bit. That's ok too! For now, I want you to write down at least 5 principles that you want to guide you on your parenting journey.

My Parenting Philosophy

_____

_____

_____

_____

_____

_____

_____

_____

_____

_____

_____

_____

_____

3

Understanding the Parent-Child Relationship

So, now that we have developed the beginnings of your very own parenting philosophy, it's time to get to work on your Parent-Child relationship. Remember that the **Parent-Child Relationship** is the bond or connection that a parent has to their child and that the child has to their parent. Another word we can use to talk about the Parent-Child relationship is *attachment*. As we move through this chapter, we'll be using *attachment* and *Parent-Child relationship* interchangeably.

In *AoP* we went into depth talking about how this relationship develops, and we tackled questions like:

- How do you nurture this relationship?
- How do you form a positive connection with your child so that your future parenting relationship with this young human being is a positive and successful one?

The simple fact is that attachment is formed by the little interactions that you have with your child. Everything counts! Big or small, everything you do from singing your child to sleep at night, to feeding them when they're hungry, to changing their diapers when they're dirty, to kissing their ouchies and owies, contributes to the Parent-Child relationship in a way that is either going to make it positive or negative.

The interesting thing about attachment is that there are "styles" of attaching. Through research, psychologists have come to identify four basic attachment styles: *Secure, Avoidant, Ambivalent,* and *Disorganized/ Disoriented.* Papalia and Feldman defined these four styles as follows:

- **Secure Attachment**- When an infant is able to to find comfort from their caregiver easily and effectively in the face of a stressful situation (214).
- **Avoidant Attachment**- A pattern of behavior where an infant rarely cries or fusses when they are separated from a caregiver, and then avoids contact or interaction with this caregiver when he/she returns to the infant (214).
- **Ambivalent/Resistant Attachment**- When an infant shows distress before a caregiver leaves them, is significantly upset while the caregiver is absent, and then wants and resists contact with their caregiver when the caregiver returns (214).
- **Disorganized/Disoriented Attachment**- In this behavioral pattern, an infant (after being left alone by the caregiver) will show different, contradictory behaviors when the caregiver returns (214).

Your goal as a parent is for your child to develop secure attachment because this reflects a sense of trust from your child. Securely attached children have learned that they can trust their caregivers, and they can trust their own ability to get their needs met.

3.1 Developing a Healthy and Secure Attachment in Children

Attachment styles begin developing early on in infancy. If and how you meet your child's needs will begin to shape the type of attachment style they develop. The more you meet your child's needs in a loving and nurturing way, the higher the chance that they develop a positive attachment style. Simple, right?

Meeting your child's needs, such as changing a dirty diaper or supporting them when they are scared at night, shows them that *you* can be trusted, that *adults* can be trusted, and that the *world* is not a scary and dangerous place. This, in turn, allows for your child to feel confident about the world they live in, and for them to feel safe enough to explore it. The key to remember here is that you need to meet their physical AND emotional needs.

If your child has one of the other attachment styles, such as *avoidant* or *disorganized*, they are not lost and gone forever! Your ability to parent your child effectively, and in a positive way, later on in their life can actually help correct these other, more problematic, attachment styles. Just because you were not the best parent when your child was an infant, does not mean that you cannot improve in your parenting and repair damage caused in the past.

The main message I want you to take away from this chapter is that a healthy Parent-Child relationship is the key to parenting success. Helping your child develop a Secure Attachment style helps to set your child up for greater success later in life. Finally, damages in the Parent-Child relationship can be remedied. Just because you made a mistake once or twice in how you interacted with your kid, does not mean that you've completely destroyed your relationship with your child. Parenting is a long-term game.

Exercise: Connect

Now that you've had some time to learn about the different attachment styles, let's make the connection and see if you can identify which attachment style your child currently has.

Go back and review the 4 attachment styles. Then, think about your child and their behavior and interactions with others. Does your child fit into one of these styles? Maybe you think they fit into 2 of these styles?

If you had to make your best guess, which attachment style would you attribute to your child? Why?

_____

_____

_____

_____

Now, I want you to consider yourself. Have you thought about what your current attachment style is? Take a second to look at those 4 styles again. Which one seems to best describe you today? Write it down.

_____

_____

_____

_____

Why do you think you have the attachment style that you do? How did your parent's actions affect your attachment style? What could they have done differently?

_____

_____

_____

_____

_____

_____

Now that you have reflected on your own attachment style and how it was impacted by your parent's actions, I want you to think back to your child. How have your actions, as a parent, impacted the current attachment style your child has? What have you done (or failed to do) that is impacting your child's attachment? If you have an infant, think about your interactions with your child. How do you think these behaviors will impact your baby's future attachment style? Write it down:

_____

_____

_____

_____

_____

_____

Was that hard to do? Were you honest with yourself? These last questions can unearth painful realities that you may have been avoiding. It's ok. The more honest you are, the better able you'll be at making the needed changes to grow as a parent.

Exercise: Respond

One of the things we learned about in this chapter is that you can make changes in your own behavior that will help to correct your child's attachment style. Look back at your answers for the last exercise. You should have written down some behaviors that are impacting your child's attachment. Answer the following question for yourself:

What is a behavior that you can begin doing today that will impact your child positively? Consider taking a behavior from the previous question that is negatively impacting your child and change it into a positive one. Here are some examples:

Example 1:

> **Current Parental Action:** I wait as long as possible to change my baby's dirty diaper.

> **New Parental Action:** I can change his diaper as soon as I notice that it is dirty.

Example 2:

> **Current Parental Action:** When my child asks if I can play with them, I try to convince them to play with a sibling instead.

> **New Parental Action:** I can stop what I'm doing and play with my child for at least 10 minutes.

Write down your new parental action:

_____

_____

_____

_____

Beginning today, do your best to remember this new action. Try your best to work on it consistently so that it becomes a habit for yourself. Whenever you feel ready, come back to this chapter and repeat the exercise with a new behavior. Repeat it as often as you need to until you are satisfied with yourself and your current parental actions. Remember, learning is doing!

4

Understanding Your
Parenting Self

In *AoP*, we took some time to really understand all the pieces that make up you as a parent. As we reviewed in Chapter 1, the *Parent* makes up a huge part of the Familial Environment, and it's important to know who you currently are as a parent in order to know who you want to become.

We all have some semblance of an idea of who we want to be as parents, and we try to manage our kids, spouses, and family life in a manner that honors this "perfect parent perception." Reality, however, loves to shove itself in the way, and that *perfect parent* rarely makes an appearance. Things start to get out of hand and a little messy, leaving us feeling flustered, overwhelmed, and burned-out. This is the time to regroup.

Whether you regroup on your own because you are a single parent, or you regroup with your co-parent, you need to push the "pause" button and take a moment to center yourself and figure everything out. This task can leave you feeling confused. One of the simplest ways of tackling this problem is to revisit who you currently are as a parent, and who it is that you hope to become. Is your initial reaction of the situation (i.e. your current parenting self) lining up with your vision of the parent you want to be (i.e. your perfect parent perception)? If it does, then awesome! You are well on your way in this journey. If it doesn't, however, how do they differ? Is there a problem with this difference?

4.1 The 4 Parenting Styles

To help you on your quest to discover who you are as a mom/dad, it might be helpful to have some understanding of what research has discovered about different parenting styles. Decades of research have concluded that there are 4 basic parenting styles:

- Permissive/Indulgent
- Authoritative
- Authoritarian
- Neglectful

Permissive is described as parents who allow their children to govern their own activities as much as possible. They give their children much power when it comes to making decisions in the home, and do not discipline their children very often. Papalia and Feldman report that these parents allow their children to govern their own activities as much as possible. They give their children much power when it comes to making decisions in the home, and do not discipline their children very often. They are warm in nature, indulgent, demand little (if anything) from their children, and are noncontrolling (301). Some experts in the field refer to this style as **Indulgent Parenting** (Santrock 77).

Authoritative is described as a parenting style that honors a child's individuality but balances it with social constraints. They implement punishment, when necessary, that is just and fair. These parents demand good behavior from their children by maintaining firm standards, but are also loving and accepting (Papalia and Feldman 301).

Authoritarian parenting is characterized by a sense of control and obedience. Authoritarian parents hold their kids to rigid behavioral standards, use punishment frequently, are less warm and more detached in the relationship with their child.

Finally, **Neglectful** is characterized by a lack of involvement. These parents rarely spend quality time with their children (Santrock 77). Parents who fall into this category know little about their children, and they fail to provide structure and/or healthy boundaries for their kids.

For the purposes of this book, we won't be looking at Neglectful Parenting. Chances are, if you're spending time reading this book, you're not a neglectful parent. Most likely, your parenting style will fall into one of the other 3 categories. As such, we are going to leave Neglectful behind and continue by examining the remaining 3 styles.

In *AoP*, we discussed viewing these styles as a continuum, with Permissive to the far left, Authoritarian to the far right, and Authoritative somewhere in the middle:

Permissive ←————————→ Authoritative ←————————→ Authoritarian

You shouldn't think of these styles as a rigid box that you either fit into or don't. You could fall anywhere, which is why I like to teach this topic to my clients as a continuum. Knowing where you lie on this continuum helps you to understand what your "default" settings are when you come up against a parenting problem, or when you are parenting from a place of distress versus from a place of calm and composure.

In *AoP*, we spent some time reviewing the pros and cons of each parenting style. It all boiled down to Authoritative being the best, producing children who are happy, self-reliant, assertive, and exhibit good self-control (Papalia and Feldman 301). As such, this is the parenting style we are going to aim for in this workbook.

Exercise: Reflect

Before you continue, I want to take a moment to process what we have just learned. Go back and review the 4 parenting styles. When you read them, make note of which one most closely resembles you and your parenting. Try to be as honest with yourself as you can. Remember, this is a private reflection. No one is going to know how you respond but you.

Were you able to identify one? Was it easy or hard to do? Write down which parenting style you identified for yourself:

_____

_____

_____

_____

Now, if you co-parent with someone, like a spouse, grandparent, etc., take a moment to reflect on what their parenting style is like. Where do they fall on that continuum? Write down the name of your co-parent and what their parenting style is. I've supplied extra space in case you have multiple co-parents.

_____

_____

_____

_____

_____

_____

Did you find it was easier to determine what your co-parent's style is as opposed to identifying your own? It's common for us to see what is happening with others because we have an "outside view" of the whole situation. As such, we aren't as clouded by emotions. When it comes time to identify our own stuff, however, that can get tricky. In my therapy office, it is rare that parents are able to identify their parenting style accurately, but they are quick to pick out the correct one for their co-parent.

Exercise: Respond

We're going to test how accurately you were able to identify your parenting style. To do this exercise, you'll need to talk to someone who knows you well as a parent. Read to them the following descriptions of the parenting styles:

- *Neglectful-* A parent who rarely attends to their child's physical and/or emotional needs. The keyword is "absent."
- *Permissive-* A parent who allows their children to govern their own activities, give their children much power, and rarely disciplines. The keyword is "freedom."
- *Authoritative-* A parent that implements just and fair punishment when necessary, but also honors their child's individuality. The keyword is "balance."
- *Authoritarian-* A parent that holds rigid behavioral standards and uses punishment frequently. The keyword is "control."

Now ask them, without thinking too much about it, what parenting style best matches you. Make sure to keep your emotions in check, and don't become defensive if the answer isn't what you expected it would be. Remember, you're doing this to learn and grow. Write down what their response is:

_____

_____

Take the opportunity to dialogue with this person about why they feel you fit this parenting style, even if it is the style you picked for yourself. Adopt a sense of curiosity and interest. Ask questions like:

- Why do you think I fit this parenting style best?
- Do I ever fit one of the other styles, such as when I'm tired, sick, or happy?
- In your opinion, do you think that this style is a good match for my kids?
- How do you think my style matches up with my co-parent's style?

Seek to learn more about yourself. You might find that this person offers great insight into who you are as a parent right now. Write down any important insights or thoughts that struck you in the dialogue you had with this person:

_____

_____

_____

_____

_____

_____

Hopefully, this exercise allowed you to learn a little more about yourself at this point in time. Feel free to repeat this exercise with others you know and trust. Each person you ask may offer newer insights, allowing you to learn more about yourself and how others see you as a parent. Remember, if you don't like the answer to these questions, you have the power to change it! That's why you're here!

4.2 The Unique Components of the Parenting You

Now that you have learned about the 3 parenting styles (excluding Neglectful), we can begin looking at the other variables that affect your parenting. There are 6 components that affect you and how you parent:

- Your Default Parenting Style
- Past Experiences
- Your Self-Esteem/ Self-Image
- Your Emotional Wellbeing/ Mental Health
- Your Personality
- Your Co-Parent

Apart from the first one, we will have a quick review of each one before we move onto our exercises. Just like in *AoP*, you'll notice many things intertwine and are interconnected. This is an important notion to remember because all parenting is this way. As we work through this workbook, you will see how everything is connected, and how rarely the answer to solving behavioral issues with children is working with the child alone. Most times, the family is key, with much of the work being done with the parent.

Past Experiences

Your past experiences will affect you and who you are as a parent. Understanding *how* it is that your past plays in who you are now is part of knowing *where* you've been. In therapy, I frequently teach individuals that understanding the "why" of something can help in identifying what needs to change. In *AoP*, we dived into some key pieces of your past that impact your parenting. They were:

- How you were raised
- Your own attachment style
- Traumatic experiences

Exercise: Reflect

Take a moment to think about your childhood. Who were the individuals that raised you? If you had to pick a parenting style for each one of them, what would it be?

_____

_____

_____

_____

_____

How do you think their parenting style impacted you? Do you think it was a good match for you and your personality or not? Why?

_____

_____

_____

_____

_____

_____

_____

If you could change anything about the relationship you had with your parents/caregivers, what would it be? Why is this important to you?

_____

_____

_____

_____

_____

Exercise: Connect

Look at your answers to the previous Reflect exercise. It's time to connect how your past is currently impacting you.

How do those things you identified in the previous exercise impact your parenting today? What do you do similarly as your parents? What do you do differently from them? Do you go to your parents for parenting advice? Why or why not?

_____

_____

_____

_____

_____

_____

_____

_____

_____

Your Self-Esteem/Self-Image

Self-esteem can be defined as the way you see yourself, whether positive or negative. A parent who has a high self-esteem is less likely to struggle with parenting. In fact, individuals with a high self-esteem are more likely to have appropriate attachment with their children, as well as utilize more authoritative parenting styles. Because they are confident in who they are, they have less of a need to seek approval or gain favor from their children, their co-parent, and/or others. They are less likely to want to be the "cool" mom or be their child's "friend."

Parents who have low self-esteem are more likely to give in to their children because there is a subconscious need to have their approval. You need to feel as though you are well-loved and well-liked. As such, you give in to your children, and are more likely to be too permissive.

A poor self-esteem can also affect your parenting in the way that you interact with your co-parent. It is not uncommon for parents to have differing parenting styles. At times, you might find a couple who agree approximately 80% of the time on how to parent their children, but seldom more than that. If you have a high self-esteem, you are less likely to struggle with issues such as challenging your co-parent on how *they* want to parent versus how *you* want to parent. You and your co-parent are more likely to discuss parenting choices and hot topics, such as discipline, in an appropriate way. Parents who have a low self-esteem will either not confront their co-parent on the issue at hand or will engage with them in an aggressive and inappropriate way.

Exercise: Reflect

We all have a generally good idea of whether or not we have a low or high self-esteem. We're going to take a moment and reflect a little deeper on how this might be impacting your parenting.

Do you have a low or high self-esteem? Circle your response:

Low Self-Esteem   High Self-Esteem

Why do you believe this to be true? What evidence supports your answer?

_____

_____

_____

_____

_____

Do you think your self-esteem is affecting your parenting? Circle your answer:

Yes   No

Why do you believe this to be true? What evidence supports your answer?

_____

_____

_____

_____

_____

_____

Your Emotional & Mental Health

In the workplace, it is common knowledge that happy employees are better and more productive. In the parenting world, it is no different. A happy mommy is a better mommy. A father who feels fulfilled in his life, is a better daddy. Being in a happy and emotionally healthy state of mind is key to, not only being the best parent that you can be, but to achieving your vision of the perfect parent. One of the most significant barriers to joyful parenting can be mental health issues, such as depression, anxiety, and trauma reactions. Any mental health condition can impact how successfully you administer discipline, engage with your children, communicate with your co-parent, and accomplish daily household tasks.

Even if a mother or father does not have a mental health condition, a parent can still be in a negative state of mind due to simple conditions that we all experience, such as stress. Stress can come from anywhere: work, home, in-laws, your family, or even your own children can cause you to feel large amounts of stress which, in turn, will affect how you parent. When you are stressed, you are more irritable, less patient, and more likely to be harsh in discipline. During times of stress or exhaustion, you are also more likely to give in to your child when they tantrum or argue with you. This, in turn, makes you less consistent as parent, and more likely to engage in, what I like to call, "couch parenting" (i.e. a parent who is giving minimal effort in parenting their child and may, literally, be sitting on a sofa, shouting directives to their child, but never actually moving from their position).

In our society today, there is a large taboo when it comes to mental health conditions. Many people suffer from a mental health disorder, but never seek help for it. This is unnecessary. There is no reason to suffer from a mental health condition when there is ample and effective help available. If you suspect that you may be suffering from a mental health disorder, please seek out help from a mental health professional, such as a marriage and family therapist.

Your Personality

Personality is a fascinating subject, and as a therapist, has been one of the most interesting things to study. For our purposes, it's important to know that personality is largely created by your genetic makeup, life experiences, and your attachment style. Your personality governs everything that you do with regard to how you interact and engage with the world. As such, your personality governs how you manage your own emotions, how you manage conflict, and how you communicate with the people around you, among other things. As such, it is easy to see how your personality would greatly affect your parenting.

Your Co-Parent

A co-parent is the person with whom you are sharing the parenting responsibilities of your children. Traditionally, co-parents are the biological mom and dad of the child, but in today's modern age, they may consist of stepparents, adoptive parents, grandparents, foster parents, daycare workers, etc. Every family is different in terms of who is sharing the responsibility to parent the children. It can be agreed, however, that your co-parent is going to affect the way that you parent. It is important that co-parents share a similar parenting vision, agreeing on how most parenting tasks will be managed in and out of the home.

Exercise: Reflect

Let's take a second to reflect on who your co-parent is as a parent. Which parenting style best reflects them? Circle the one that best represents them:

- *Neglectful-* A parent who rarely attends to their child's physical and/or emotional needs. The keyword is "absent."
- *Permissive-* A parent who allows their children to govern their own activities, give their children much power, and rarely disciplines. The keyword if "freedom."
- *Authoritative-* A parent that implements just and fair punishment when necessary, but also honors their child's individuality. The keyword is "balance."
- *Authoritarian-* A parent that holds rigid behavioral standards and uses punishment frequently. The keyword is "control."

How does this match with your parenting? Are they the same or different? If they are different, how *much* different are they? Write down some brief reflections on this.

_____

_____

_____

_____

_____

_____

Exercise: Connect

Now that you've identified your parenting style and that of your partners, let's compare how these work together and/or against each other. Let's look at an example:

Parenting Combination: Permissive and Authoritarian

> **Pros:** It can be said that this combination balances each other out. On one end of the spectrum, you have a harsh disciplinarian who is probably considered the "enforcer" within the parenting team. On the other spectrum, you have a permissive parent that gives the children more liberty and provides space for individuality and freedom. This parent is probably considered the "fun parent" in this duo. Because of this balance, you may not see as many negative effects of these parenting styles on the kids.[1]

> **Cons:** These parents are not on the same page and probably experience much bickering behind closed doors. They disagree constantly on how to parent the kids and this (most likely) leads to strain on their relationship. Furthermore, some children might take advantage of the permissive parent and may not have respect for this parent due to their leniency.

Take a moment and consider the pros and cons of your parenting combination. In what ways does it work well and in what ways does it create difficulty? How does your parenting combination affect your relationship with your partner? How does it affect your kids?

Pros

_____

_____

_____

_____

_____

_____

Cons

_____

_____

_____

_____

_____

_____

Your Parenting Style & Your Child: The Goodness of Fit

Goodness of Fit is a concept that has to do with how appropriate an environment matches a child. Essentially, does the child and his personality match the demands of his or her environment, or does the parent (and who that parent is) match up well with the child, and who that child is. It should be noted that a child and a parent do not need to be a perfect match. The better the match, however, the more likely that the parent and the child will have a strong, healthy, and positive Parent-Child relationship.

Who you are as a person (i.e. your personality, your parenting style, your attachment style) will either line up with who your child is or it won't. Your child's temperament and personality may be at complete odds with who you are as a parent, and as such, parenting this child will be much more challenging for you. On the other hand, if who you are lines up with who your child is, then you will find that your ability to parent this child seems to come naturally because the fit between you and your child is a good match.

Exercise: Reflect

This exercise is simple enough but will, hopefully, be thought provoking. Reflect on the following questions and then write down your response. If you have multiple children, answer these questions for each child.

Are you and your child a "good fit" for one another? Why or why not?

_____

_____

_____

_____

_____

_____

4.3 Moving On

Over the course of these last few chapters, we have been building a thorough understanding of who *you* are as a parent, as well as the different components that are coming together to create your current parenting-self. Hopefully, you have come to see parenting is like a giant, intricately designed spider web, where everything is connected to everything else, and changing or altering one part of the web will most certainly affect the rest of it. Parenting is far from being one dimensional! You must have a firm understanding of how all of these pieces come together to create the picture that is you and your current family system. In doing this, you'll be better able to see where the "hiccups" are, and thus, better able to formulate and implement change.

[1] In *AoP*, we reviewed what research has identified as effects from the different parenting styles. It is recommended that you re-read that section to help you with this exercise in identifying pros and cons.

5

Your Parent-Child Relationship & How to Improve It

5.1 The Power of Human Connection

A strong Parent-Child relationship offers many benefits to you and your child. Research has shown that a positive relationship can increase communication between you and your child, decrease hostility and aggression in children, and improve their social skills. It can decrease the possibility of drug use by teens, decrease problematic behaviors, and potentially increase self-esteem. Furthermore, as if these benefits weren't enough, a strong, positive Parent-Child relationship offers a protective factor against mental health conditions such as depression and anxiety, as well as serious risk behaviors such as suicide and non-suicidal self-harm (such as cutting).

In *AoP*, I shared a story about my client, Eric. The human connection I had developed with him, was so strong, so powerful, and so positive in his life, that it saved him. The story demonstrated how a positive relationship with your child can make all the difference in the choices that they make. The power of human connection is one of the strongest and most effective tools I have as a therapist, and it's one of the most important tools you have as a parent. It's necessary to note that connection with your child is a life-long process. Once you've built it up, you need to nurture it consistently over time. The work is never truly done.

So, now that we have an understanding about how important this relationship truly is, the time has come to begin discussing how we create it, on a continuous basis, throughout the lifespan of your child.

5.2 How to Create a Strong, Positive Relationship with Your Child

What I would like to teach you is what I like to call the "Emotional Piggy Bank." At this point, we already know how to create a healthy attachment with infants, but as children grow older, the Parent-Child relationship can become more difficult to manage and nurture. That is what this chapter is all about. To begin, let's discuss what the Emotional Piggy Bank is.

The Emotional Piggy Bank

The **Emotional Piggy Bank** is how relationships work. Imagine a bank account, except that this is an *emotional* bank account. Every relationship you have has its own separate account that you share with them (i.e. one account for you and your spouse, a second account for you and your child, a third account for your spouse and your child). Every time you engage with a person in a positive way, you are depositing funds into your emotional bank account with that particular person. Every time you engage in an argument or do something that offends or hurts the other person, you are withdrawing funds from that emotional bank account. The more funds you deposit, the wealthier your account becomes. The more funds you withdraw from the account, the poorer your account becomes. As with your real bank accounts, your goal should always be to be in the black, with sufficient funds in your account to live comfortably. No one likes to be in debt, and so the same principle is true of the Emotional Piggy Bank.

Building a positive Parent-Child relationship, is all about continuously depositing funds into the Emotional Piggy Bank that you share with your child. Every time you reprimand them, discipline them, yell at them, etc., you are withdrawing funds from that account. Every time you engage with them in a way that is nourishing and positive, you deposit funds into the account. Depending on your child's age, how you nurse the relationship will be different. If you have an infant, feeding them, singing to them, rocking them, and so on, are all ways you would deposit funds. If you have a toddler, playing peek-a-boo with them, or swinging them at a park, are ways that you may engage with them to deposit funds. If you have a teenager, going out together for a bite to eat, or seeing a movie together, cooking together, working on a car together, supporting them at their baseball games, and so forth, are all ways that you may be able to deposit funds into your emotional bank account. Essentially, the more quality time you have with your child, the richer that account becomes. The richer your account becomes, the more the account can withstand hardship. So, if your teen decides to lie to you, and you and your teen have a huge, blowout argument, you will be making a huge withdrawal from the account. But, because the account was so rich to begin with, it can withstand this large withdrawal and, as such, does not go into the red. These are the basics for developing a positive Parent-Child relationship.

Creating a "Rich" Emotional Bank Account

There are many ways to create a "rich" emotional bank account. I'll spend some time and discuss 3 of them, elaborating and helping you to really understand how these items come together to make for a positive

Parent-Child relationship. In this section, the 3 items we will be looking at are:

- Quality Time
- Family Narrative
- Admitting Parental Failure

Quality Time

As I have already hinted, one of the best ways to begin building a rich emotional bank account with your child is by spending lots of quality time with them. I define **Quality time** as spending time engaging in an activity that the other person enjoys. That means that, in order for your activity to "count" as quality time, and thus, "deposit" funds into that account, it must be something your child enjoys too! There are tons of ways to engage in quality time, you just need to get creative and make this a priority! Regular family time creates a positive family narrative and culture. Consistent time spent together helps to create and improve the Parent-Child relationship. This is done by creating positive interactions between siblings and caregivers.

Exercise: Reflect

Take a moment to think of the last time you had "quality time" with your child. Use this interaction to answer the following questions. Remember to be honest with yourself. You won't benefit from the exercise if you're not honest in your responses.

When you last interacted with your child, what was the interaction like for *you?*

Positive   Neutral   Negative

During the interaction, were you checking your phone, watching your favorite TV show, talking to someone else, etc.?

Yes   No

How long did your interaction last (in minutes)?

5   10   15   20   25   30+

Did you have to scold your child or discipline them during the interaction?

Yes   No

What do you think the interaction was like for your child?

Positive   Neutral   Negative

Exercise: Connect

Sometimes, we think we are giving our children great quality time, but the truth may be a hard reality to swallow. When you look back on your answers, what do you notice? How engaged were you *really* with your child? If you answered that "Yes" to the second question in the *Reflect* exercise, then you might not have been giving your children *quality* time. Yes, you might have been spending time with them, but it was distracted, with part of your time being engaged with something else. Let's look at an example to explore this further.

Example:

Mary has decided to sit down with her son, Greg, to have quality time. They are playing a game. While they are playing, Greg is telling her about his day at school.

"And then, I hit the ball so hard that the goalie couldn't catch it! So, I won the game for the team. It was so awesome!"

Mary smiles at him, "That's great," she replies as she checks her messages again on her phone.

Greg feels a stab in his chest as he thinks to himself, *Why are you always looking at your phone, Mom. Pay attention! I'm trying to tell you something important.* He tries to shake the thought from his mind and tries to engage her again. "So, the Coach said that I should try out for the soccer team. He thinks I'm really good, and that I could really help the team this year."

Mary, still looking at her phone, "That could be fun."

Greg's eyebrows furrow a bit. *Did she even hear what I just said? They want me to play on the team!* Annoyed and hurt, he decides to take a different approach. "So, what you looking at on your phone, Mom?"

"Hmm? What did you ask?" She asks, looking up from her phone.

"What are you looking at?"

"Oh! I was reading my newsfeed. Why do you ask?"

The familiar stabbing pain returns to Greg's chest. *Is your stupid newsfeed more important than me?* "Nothing... just curious."

Getting a snapshot of Greg's inner thoughts helps us to interpret how Greg is experiencing this interaction. Although Mary has great intentions, and she is trying to spend time with her son, we can see that Greg's experience is not a positive one. He is feeling unheard and unimportant. In the end, this quality time isn't really *quality* at all.

Considering this example, I want you to think about the interaction you were using in the *Reflect* exercise. I asked, "What do you think the interaction was like for your child?" I'm going to ask you the same question again, but this time, I want you to consider your child's experience a little deeper. Think about Greg in our example. Do you think your child may have had thoughts like Greg's? Do you think your child would say that the interaction was truly *quality* time? Think on this for a moment. Now, respond....

What do you think the interaction was like for your child?

Positive   Neutral   Negative

Did your answer remain the same or did it change? If you truly feel your child had a positive experience from the interaction, then that's great! You want to begin having more of these positive interactions together. If you think the interaction was neutral or negative, then we have some room for improvement.

Exercise: Respond

Regardless of how you would rate the quality of your interactions with your child, our children can always benefit from an increase in quality time. Although some of us might be very good at giving our children true, *quality* time, we do it too infrequently. In this exercise, we're going to work on boosting that a bit.

Take a look at your schedule for the week and see if you can set aside at least 10 minutes every day to spend with each one of your children. If you have 2 kids, then you would be giving 10 minutes to one child and 10 minutes to another, for a total of 20 minutes each day. In this interaction, engage in an activity of your child's choosing. During your interactions with your child, try to show a sincere interest in the activities they have chosen. Be sure to turn off the TV, put away tablets, cell phones, and computers and truly give your child your undivided attention for at least 10 minutes.

During this time, show a sincere interest in what they're doing by providing enthusiastic commentary or positive statements about the activity they are engaging in. For example, if your child has decided to color with you, perhaps praise their use of color, or comment on how well they have drawn a tree or a person. Allow your child the opportunity to lead the activity and try to refrain from making suggestions, asking questions, and/or criticizing your child.

I want you to try this for one week. As you go along your week, take note of how your child responds to you by the end of the week. Do they seem happier to see you? Are they more excited when you come home from work? Do they seem more animated when talking to you? Write down your observations.

_____

_____

_____

_____

_____

_____

_____

Hopefully, you see a positive reaction from your child. The more time you spend with them in quality time, the better your Parent-Child relationship will become! Now, it's important to note that 10 minutes a day shouldn't be the *only* time you engage with your child.

You should be engaging with them constantly throughout the day and week. Whether it's sitting at the dinner table talking about the day or helping them with their homework, you should be spending more than just 10 minutes with your kids. The idea here is for that dedicated, uninterrupted time with each child, so that each child can feel the love you have for them, demonstrated by your undivided time and attention. If you can muster more than 10 minutes, even better!

Now, if your child is not used to getting this kind of attention from you, you might find that your child starts acting up. This is because your child isn't used to getting this type of interaction from you. If this happens, try the following:

- Ignore the negative behavior by looking away or simply not responding to it.
- Refrain from scolding or lecturing your child. Doing this may backfire by providing attention for misbehavior. This, inadvertently, rewards the negative behavior.
- If your child continues being disruptive (or dangerous) during the one-on-one time, stop the one-on-one time for that day. By doing this, you are sending the message to your child, that engaging in negative behavior results in no attention from you.

Overtime, as you consistently spend these 10 minutes a day with your child, you will see a decrease in negative behaviors and an increase in positive behaviors. They begin to see that engaging in "good" behavior gets attention from you and "negative" behavior results in no attention.

For busy parents, it's hard to find those 10 minutes a day for every child. There are many ways you can creatively spend positive time with your child while also taking care of your daily tasks. If this is an area you struggle with, consider checking out my other book, *Trials of the Working Parent,* where I go into much more detail on how to increase quality time with your children while also managing daily life. You can also visit my website (kcdreisbach.com) where I have several articles tackling this topic.

Family Narrative

A **family narrative** is the story of your family, as told by any given person in your family. It is the perspective of that particular person. For example, when I think of my family, I recall hundreds of positive stories. Occasionally, I might think of a sad event, such as a death, or of an argument that was particularly rough, but, overall, the memories are bright and happy. Furthermore, when I imagine the different members in my family, positive descriptions come to mind because I see them all as wonderful people. Since the stories I remember and the adjectives I would use to describe my family members are all strongly positive, then I most likely have a positive family narrative. If, when I tell the story of my family, I talk about how angry my dad always was, how much my brother and sister fought all the time, and how I spent most of my time alone in my room, etc., then my family narrative is more bleak and more negative. The goal is for you to develop, and help your child develop, a positive and happy family narrative.

I'm going to take some time to explain why this is important. In depression there is a theory on how to treat depression by using something called "behavioral activation." The theory is that when people become depressed, they begin to isolate, and they start to view the world in a negative way because they are sad. The more they isolate, the less they do the things that they once used to enjoy. The less they do the things that they once used to enjoy, the fewer memories they have of joyful things. The more time they spend alone and sad, the more memories they have of being alone and sad. What ends up happening is that the narrative of their life becomes a story about depression; a story about being depressed and alone. This, in turn, feeds back into the depression causing a vicious cycle that makes the person spiral further and further down into that depressed state.

With **behavioral activation**, the therapist assigns the client activities to do that are supposed to help increase positive memories for the client. Activities might be to go for a walk with a friend, to call a friend and talk to them about a movie, to go out to dinner with a spouse, and so on. The principle behind behavioral activation is that, as the client engages in more and more activities that he enjoys and likes, he begins to form more memories that are positive. The more positive memories he forms, the less his story becomes about depression (Selva, *Behavioural Activation*). The less his story becomes about depression, the more joy he is going to feel, and the less depressed he will become. This, in turn, causes the client to begin reversing that spiral, spiraling up and out of depression.

When we talk about positive family narratives, we are essentially using the same idea behind behavioral activation. By creating and engaging in various activities that are positive to the people involved, we are helping the child and the parent to develop positive memories which, in turn, creates a positive family narrative. This means that we are depositing lots of funds into the emotional bank account.

Exercise: Reflect

Think back to your own childhood. What are the adjectives you would use to describe it? Consider some of the following words and circle the ones you feel apply to the family narrative of your childhood:

Sad   Joyful   Jealousy   Abusive   Happy   Scary   Hurt

Scattered   Sickening   Ugly   Beautiful   Trusting   Loss

Angry   Funny   Fun   Adventurous   Boring   Big   Small

Lost   Lonely   Companionship   Generous   Spiritual

Stingy   Poor   Rich   Painful   Close   Distant   Positive

Negative   Neutral   Separate   Together   Understanding

Compassionate   Bitter   Misunderstood   Unloved   Loved

When you look back at all of the words you circled, what do you notice? Are there any commonalities among the words you selected? Are they primarily positive or negative? Does anything surprise you? By selecting the words that best reflect the narrative for your childhood family's story, you have a better grasp of whether your story is a positive or negative one.

Exercise: Connect

Now, I want you to close your eyes and put yourself in your child's shoes. Try to imagine your *current* family through the eyes of your child. Remember our example of Mary and Greg. Try to adopt your child's attitude and circle the words you think your child would use to describe their family at this current point in time:

Sad   Joyful   Jealousy   Abusive   Happy   Scary   Hurt

Scattered   Sickening   Ugly   Beautiful   Trusting   Loss

Angry   Funny   Fun   Adventurous   Boring   Big   Small

Lost   Lonely   Companionship   Generous   Spiritual

Stingy   Poor   Rich   Painful   Close   Distant   Positive

Negative   Neutral   Separate   Together   Understanding

Compassionate   Bitter   Misunderstood   Unloved   Loved

Looking back at your answers, what do you notice? Are their primarily positive, negative, or neutral words? Was this difficult for you? Did you find yourself warring with what you wanted to circle versus what you believe your child would actually circle? What insights, if any, did you glean for this exercise? Take a moment to write down any important thoughts about Family Narrative's that came to mind as you completed the *Reflect* and *Connect* exercises. What did you learn?

_____

_____

_____

_____

_____

_____

_____

Family Narratives are an important part of the puzzle and they go hand-in-hand with quality time. The more time you spend engaging with your children teaching them, talking to them, listening to them, playing with them, mentoring them, modeling for them, and just giving them your time, the better and more positive your Family's Narrative will become.

If you are interested in more help on Family Narrative, feel free to visit my website at kcdreisbach.com/blog for articles, tips, and advice on creating a healthy and positive family culture.

Exercise: Respond

This exercise is intended for parents with older kids. For those of you with pre-verbal children, you can always flag this one and try it out when your child is older.

If you have an older child, you're going to test out how well you predicted the words your child would use to describe the family. Find some time this week where you and your child can be alone. Perhaps go out for a walk, have a picnic, or go to lunch together. Then, read the directions below to your child and circle the words they endorse.

Directions: I'm going to read to you some words and I want you to tell me which ones you would use to describe our family. I want you to try and be as honest as possible. Don't worry about hurting my feelings or making me feel bad. Are you ready?

Sad   Joyful   Jealousy   Abusive   Happy   Scary   Hurt

Scattered   Sickening   Ugly   Beautiful   Trusting   Loss

Angry   Funny   Fun   Adventurous   Boring   Big   Small

Lost   Lonely   Companionship   Generous   Spiritual

Stingy   Poor   Rich   Painful   Close   Distant   Positive

Negative   Neutral   Separate   Together   Understanding

Compassionate   Bitter   Misunderstood   Unloved   Loved

When your child is done, ask them if they want to talk about the words they selected. If they say "no," don't push it! Respect their choice not to discuss what they have selected. If they want to, then practice your listening skills and just *listen.* Try your best to refrain from arguing, interrogating, or asking too many questions, especially if the words they selected are not positive ones. Let your child lead this discussion. Just listen and absorb! If you ask too many questions, try to debate your child, or try to point out to them how the family's story is different than what they chose, your child WILL SHUT DOWN (very common with teens!). This is the opposite of what you want. Make an effort to speak minimally and take note of any reasons they give you of why they feel this way:

_____

_____

_____

_____

_____

_____

_____

_____

What was it like to do this exercise? Did you find that you and your child used similar words to describe the family? If so, that's great! It means you have a decent understanding of how your child is interpreting the events in your family. If this wasn't the case for you, that's ok too! It's hard to really know what your child is thinking. We aren't mind readers! Furthermore, as we go through the various exercises of this workbook, you're going to find that you will begin to understand your child's perspective more and become more attuned with them, which will help to boost your Parent-Child relationship! For now, hang tight and keep steady the course.

Admitting Parental Failure

As human beings, we all make mistakes, but being able to admit we're wrong is huge. Making mistakes as a parent can withdraw funds from that emotional bank account, but you can help replace those funds by admitting you've made a mistake. This can be very hard to do.

For most folks, it is difficult to admit you're wrong or to admit that you have made a mistake. Pride often gets in the way of this. Being able to admit that you made a mistake to your child can not only assist in depositing depleted funds from your Emotional Piggybank, but it can also assist in healing and repairing a damaged Parent-Child relationship. Furthermore, it models to your child how to take responsibility for one's actions. Moreover, if you, as a parent, can go a step further and ask for forgiveness from your child, you will model to them a lesson in humility.

Asking our children for forgiveness, and admitting when we have made a mistake, can be an invaluable teaching tool. Just like we discussed earlier in this book, the way you interact with your child serves as a model to your child about how he or she should interact with the world. That is why it is so important for us to model to our children the behaviors we want to see in them. If you want a child who is compassionate, then you must show them compassion. If you want a child who values forgiveness, then you must ask and give forgiveness. If you want a child who uses their words in a calm manner when upset, then you must use your words in a calm manner when you are upset.

Another important note to make is that you must give your child the opportunity to share his own emotions when you are admitting parental failure. If you go to your child, tell them you made a mistake and are asking for forgiveness, you must be prepared for your child to tell you that they do not forgive you, or that they're hurt by what you have done. These are not easy things to hear, nor are they pleasant to

deal with. You must be able to tolerate them. This is extremely important. In life, we all have to deal with news that is not pleasant, and in
tolerating this type of news from your child, you are, once again, modeling to them how to accept the negative in a gracious way.

Finally, when it comes to admitting parental failure, you should do
this no matter how old your child is. Whether you are holding an infant in your arms or they're 18-years-old, when you make a mistake,
admit it, and ask for forgiveness. It's common for parents to forget that
their infant deserves to hear these words too. A parent may recognize
that what they did or said to the baby was wrong but then fail to take
that extra step to apologize. It might seem silly, but this is important
for a variety of reasons:

1. Your infant is listening. They may not fully understand you
   yet, but they can interpret facial expressions and your tone of
   voice. These things help to carry your message to them, even
   if they can't understand your words.
2. Beginning this practice when your child is an infant helps to
   stretch and exercise these "parenting muscles." For some of us,
   this practice is going to be really hard to do. So, start practicing early on before your child has the ability to verbally respond to your request for forgiveness. The more you practice,
   the easier it will get.
3. If you have adopted principle 7 from my parenting philosophy
   (i.e. *The core of the Parent-Child relationship must be in respect.*),
   then you are truly living this principle, showing your infant
   from the very beginning that they are deserving and worthy of
   respect.

Exercise: Respond

Take a moment and think about the past 7 days. Is there anything
that you did to your child that you should apologize for? Consider
some of these situations:

- Forgetting something important for your child
- Striking your child out of anger or frustration
- Calling your child a name or demeaning them in some way (i.e. *Why did you do that? That was so stupid of you.*)
- Screaming at your child without reason (usually because you are already upset about something else)
- Not listening to your child when they are speaking to you (Remember Mary and Greg!)
- Failing to acknowledge your child's accomplishments and/or hard work
- Using fear as a way to force obedience from your child (i.e. *If you don't do this, then I'm going to hit you.*)

None of us are perfect, and we are all going to make mistakes at some point or another. Even the best parenting expert is going to mess up sometimes. This book isn't about shaming or making you feel like a failure. It's about helping you to learn, evolve, and grow into the best parent that you can be! And remember, no one is seeing your answers but you. So you can be completely honest with yourself without fear of judgement from anyone!

Now that you have identified a situation where you should apologize to your child, I want you to specifically write down what you think you need to apologize for. For example, there might be a situation where you scolded your child for their behavior. You may not want to apologize for scolding your child, but you may want to apologize for the way in which you scolded them (i.e. you called them "stupid" or perhaps you were harsher than the situation required, etc.). Take a moment to think through the situation and clearly identify what you need to apologize for and write it down:

_____

_____

_____

_____

Now that you know exactly what you need to apologize for, it's time to put our learning into action. Find sometime this week where you can be alone with your child. Then, you're going to apologize for what happened. If you're not too sure how to begin this conversation, don't worry! I got you covered. I'm going to give you my Apology Recipe that you can follow. I'll also give you some sample language to use too! Remember Mary and Greg? We're going to use them again to help you practice the Apology Recipe.

The Apology Recipe

1. Begin by reminding your child about the situation that occurred.

   Sample: "Greg, do you remember the other day when you were talking to me about soccer and I was on my phone?"

2. Once your child remembers the situation, identify that you need to apologize to them, what you are apologizing for, and why you need to apologize.

   Sample: "I need to apologize to you. You were trying to tell me something that was important to you, and I wasn't giving you my full attention. I need to apologize for that. Just like I want you to pay attention to me when I am talking to you, I need to do the same for you."

3. Then, deliver a sincere apology and ask for forgiveness.

   Sample: "I'm sorry that I wasn't fully listening to you when you were speaking to me, Greg. Will you forgive me?"

4. Assuming your child forgives you (and they usually do), acknowledge their forgiveness with gratitude. If your child doesn't forgive you (it's rare but it happens), acknowledge and respect that they aren't ready to grant you forgiveness.

> *Sample 1: Forgiveness Granted* - "Thank you for forgiving me, Greg. I really appreciate it."

> *Sample 2: Forgiveness Denied* - "I understand that you're not ready to forgive me, and that's ok. Whenever you are ready, let me know, ok?"

5. Let your child know your specific plan to improve your behavior next time.

> *Sample:* "I'm going to do my very best to do better. Next time you want to talk to me about something important, I'm going to put my phone away so I don't get distracted by it. If I forget to put my phone away, would you please remind me?"

Notice that Mary is giving Greg some power by enlisting his help. This shows your child that you are truly invested in improving. This is not required, but it is a nice touch.

6. Finish with an affirmation and Act of Love (a physical gesture of affection that helps to repair any damage caused to the Parent-Child relationship). Consider gestures such as a handshake, hug, kiss, or even pat on the back. The important part is to use physical touch as a repair agent in the relationship.

> *Sample:* "I love you, Greg. Don't you ever forget that." Mary then pulls her son in for a firm embrace.

Some families struggle with physical gestures of love, such as hugs and kisses. Although I really recommend this step, it's ok if you can't do this part. At minimum, reaffirm your love to your child, even if you can't seal it with physical affection.

That's the Apology Recipe! Now it's your turn to try it out. You've already identified what you need to apologize for, now go and do it! Once completed, take a moment to reflect on the experience. What was it like to apologize to your child? How did it all go? How did your child respond? Gather any insights you gained for this experience and log them now:

_____

_____

_____

_____

_____

_____

_____

5.3 Damaging the Parent-Child Relationship & How to Repair It

As rich as your Emotional Piggy Bank may be, there is always a possibility that it becomes damaged over time. Just like any relationship, as humans, we make mistakes that can affect the relationship, and sometimes, those mistakes may be way too big, causing a rich account to become entirely depleted in one big swoop!

A damaged Parent-Child relationship is one in which there is an overdraft of funds pulled from the Emotional Piggy Bank. The most obvious causes to a damaged relationship are forms of child abuse, such as sexual abuse, physical abuse, neglect, and emotional/psychological abuse. Engaging in activities that can be considered abusive are highly damaging to the Parent-Child relationship and have a high likelihood of causing mental health issues and behavioral problems in children. If you suspect that you or someone you know might be engaging in abusive behaviors, please consider consulting with a family therapist to discuss how to address these issues in your home.

Another way that the Parent-Child relationship can become damaged (i.e. an overdraft of the emotional bank account) is when you have a parent who's emotional well-being has been impacted negatively in some way. I'm sure you have heard of the title "Angry Mommy," which usually references a parent who is seemingly angry *all* the time. It's typically a mother or father who is highly stressed, overwhelmed, and in need of a big break!

Apart from being stressed, mental health issues can also cause parents to be emotionally unavailable to the child. This can be due to past trauma (for the parent), or insecurities leading to low self-esteem, compromising the parent's ability to manage or handle the child's emotions. These items can also lead to a parent failing to create a positive family narrative. The good news is that the damage caused to a Parent-Child relationship can always be repaired!

As mentioned previously, the key to a strong Parent-Child relationship is a strong and positive family narrative. Building memories with your child and responding to your child's needs are one of the important ways of repairing the damaged relationship.

Exercise: Reflect

Now that you know all about the Emotional Piggy Bank, you need to take the time to evaluate how your account currently looks. Are you in the positive? Are you in the negative? Is it neutral? Assess your emotional bank account for each one of your children. Based off of everything you have learned in this chapter, why do you think your account is this way?

_____

_____

_____

_____

_____

_____

Remember that whether your account is currently rich or depleted, it will vary. It will change over time depending on the choices you make as a parent. This is great news because it means that you have the power to improve the relationship you currently have with your child no matter where it's at!

Exercise: Connect

Take a moment to go back and re-read your response to the *Family Narrative Connect* exercise or the *Family Narrative Respond* exercise. In these exercises, you either imagined what words your child would use to describe your family's story, or you actually asked your child what words they would select. You just need to pick one of these exercises. If you were able to complete the *Respond* exercise, then this is the one I would recommend using. If you didn't do that one, use *Connect.*

In looking back on this exercise, how does it match up with your opinion on the health of your emotional bank account? Circle the one that most applies to you:

Both are Positive   Both are Negative

Both are Neutral   They are Different

For example, if you believe your Emotional Piggy Bank is in the positive, are the words your child would use to describe their family *also* positive? If the words they would use to describe their family are negative, did you also assess that your emotional bank account is *also* in the negative?

Typically, your assessment of your emotional bank account and the words your child would use to describe their narrative would match. There are times, however, where there might be a discrepancy. This is not as common, but it can happen. I usually see this when there is a negative family narrative due to abuse from one parent, but a positive emotional bank account with the other parent.

Take just a few minutes to write down why you believe your emotional bank account matches or differs from the words your child would use to describe your family's narrative.

_____

_____

_____

_____

Through this exercise, I'm hoping you were able to see the connection between the family narrative and the health of your Emotional Piggy Bank. They go hand-in-hand.

No matter where your account is at, you can always repair it and/or improve it by creating positive family memories. This will help in building a positive family narrative. If you remember earlier in this chapter, we discussed behavioral activation, and how it brings people back from depression. Similar to behavioral activation, your family narrative is the way that you can bring your relationship back into a positive state and maintain it with a healthy balance. Always remember that the family narrative is the key to a happy family.

Exercise: Respond, Part 1

Time to roll up those sleeves and get to doing! Right now, we're going to brainstorm ways that you can improve your family narrative. For the purpose of this exercise, we're going to focus on activities. Earlier in this chapter, I asked you to increase your quality time with your child. Hopefully, you did it and saw a positive result! I'm going to ask you to do this again, but this time, we're going to dedicate more than just 10 minutes.

For this exercise, I want you to identify one morning, afternoon, or evening each week where you can dedicate time to your kids. We're looking for a few hours here (if possible). During this time, you are going to engage in some serious quality time! Here are some examples:

- Game Night on Friday evening- Play video games or board games together as a family for a few hours
- Movie Night- Go out to the movies, rent a movie, or watch a family favorite at home together
- Picnic at the Park- Go on a family picnic once a week
- Family Hike- Enjoy a hike in the local woods as a family once a week
- Family Walk- Take a minimum of a 30-minute walk around the neighborhood
- Outdoor Play Date- Block an hour (or more!) to play outside with your kids on swings, playing tag, or doing a scavenger hunt for natural materials such as leaves, rocks, etc.
- Family Hide-N-Seek- Take turns hiding and looking for each other (you can do this one outside or in your home)

- Family Drive- Take a scenic drive into the mountains, to the beach, to the city, or anywhere near you that offers a fun driving experience
- Craft Night- Using materials in your house (like empty tissue boxes), create something new

I hope this list got your creative juices flowing. Now it's your turn! Think of something you would like to try with your family. Carve out 1 day each week for the next 4 weeks that you are going to try and implement this. Ideally, we want your co-parent to join in on the fun. If that's not possible, then move forward with just yourself and your kids. Once you've completed the exercise, I want you to reflect on the experience. Consider some of these questions in your reflection:

- What was it like?
- Did your children enjoy themselves?
- How do you feel about yourself, as a parent, after the experience? Perhaps more attuned, less guilty, or maybe the same as before?
- If your co-parent joined in, what was it like to have that parent involved in the activities?

Write down some of the thoughts you had about this experience.

_____

_____

_____

_____

_____

_____

Now, if your children are old enough (probably about 3 or older), I want you to ask your kids about what they thought. Consider questions such as:

- Did you like getting to spend time as a family to do these activities?
- Did you have fun doing these things as a family?
- What was your favorite part?
- Is there anything you didn't like? Why?
- If we could keep doing these things once a week, would you like that? Why?

Remember to make your questions age-appropriate and remember that your child's answer will vary greatly depending on their age. Write down the things they shared with you about the experience.

_____

_____

_____

_____

_____

Hopefully, your children enjoyed the extra time with you. Children (even teenagers) love spending time with their parents in fun activities (even if the teens try to pretend that they don't!). Let's say, however, that your children didn't enjoy the experience. Perhaps it was a miserable time for you all. If this was the case, we need to take a closer look at what went wrong.

At this time, if your children didn't enjoy the family time, and you believe this experiment did not work out, write down what went wrong. Include your thoughts about "why" you think this exercise didn't go well. We'll look at this in a future section of this workbook, so don't skip it if the exercise didn't go well. (If your family had a positive experience from this exercise, you can skip this part.)

_____

_____

_____

_____

_____

_____

_____

Exercise: Respond, Part 2

Now that you've completed Part 1 of this exercise, we're going to re-evaluate how your child would describe your family's narrative. Find some time (preferably today or tomorrow) to sit down with them. Just like before, read the directions off to them and then circle the words your child endorses.

Directions: I'm going to read to you some words and I want you to tell me which ones you would use to describe our family. I want you to try and be as honest as possible. Don't worry about hurting my feelings or making me feel bad. Are you ready?

Sad   Joyful   Jealousy   Abusive   Happy   Scary   Hurt

Scattered   Sickening   Ugly   Beautiful   Trusting   Loss

Angry   Funny   Fun   Adventurous   Boring   Big   Small

Lost   Lonely   Companionship   Generous   Spiritual

Stingy   Poor   Rich   Painful   Close   Distant   Positive

Negative   Neutral   Separate   Together   Understanding

Compassionate   Bitter   Misunderstood   Unloved   Loved

When your child is done, ask them if they want to talk about the words they selected. Just like before, if they say "no," don't push it. We want to respect their choice not to discuss what they have selected. Make sure you listen and refrain from arguing, interrogating, or asking too many questions, especially if the words they selected are not positive ones. Let your child lead this discussion. Write down some of the key points they share with you.

Take a moment now to review the words they selected and what thoughts they had on the experience. Compare their responses this time around with the ones you received previously. Are there any differences? Did your child select more positive words this time? Are there more neutral or negative ones this time? Write down what you noticed in your comparison.

_____

_____

_____

_____

_____

_____

Hopefully, your child's narrative is beginning to shift from negative to neutral or from neutral to positive. If your child's narrative was already positive, it should have stayed that way. The purpose of the exercise was to help demonstrate how increasing quality time shifts the family narrative into a positive place and improves the Parent-Child relationship.

Regardless of the current status of your Emotional Piggy Bank, you can use this exercise (Part 1 and Part 2) to continuously improve your Parent-Child relationship and assess the current status of your family narrative through the eyes of your children. If you and your family had a positive experience from this exercise, I encourage you to keep reserving 1 day each week to engage in a family activity.

6

Understanding Psychological Development in Children

I am a big believer of the old adage, "Knowledge is Power." I think this is particularly true when we talk about understanding our children and why they behave the way that they do. Frequently, comprehending the root cause (or the "why") of behavior helps parents to better identify what they can do to help support positive changes in their child. As such, this chapter is designed to help you understand your child's psychological, social, and emotional development from infancy to early adulthood.

In order to make this chapter more manageable, it will be broken down into a few sections: infancy (0 to 3 years of age), early childhood (approximately 3 years to 6 years of age), middle childhood (from about 6 to 11 years of age), and adolescence (from about 12 to 20 years of age).

I'm going to give you a basic understanding of what your child is going through at different developmental stages. It should be a rough sketch of what is going on in your child's mind while providing you with some foundational knowledge we can use in future discussions about behaviors and behavioral change in later chapters.

6.1 Development in Infancy

During the first three years of life, the psychosocial and physical development of children is fast and significant. In just three short years, children go from immobile entities who are 100% dependent on their caregivers, to unique individuals who have their own needs, wants, and plans. This age group also presents one of the more challenging times in the Parent-Child relationship... the Terrible Twos! Since development during these years are so impactful, it's a good idea to further break down this age range, looking at each year of life to better understand what is going on in our children's hearts and minds.

Birth to 12 Months

From the very beginning, children have their own personalities. Although there are many common behaviors that are similar in infants, such as basic sucking reflexes, babies still show signs of their own, unique personality as early as the first few days of life. If you are a parent of multiple kids, you can vouch for this statement! Some infants are "easy babies," eat lazily, or spend most days sleeping. Others might be described as "difficult babies" or colicky, requiring constant rocking in order to soothe them. My own children were (and still are) at opposite ends of the personality spectrum. Still, despite these differences, all children will master different social skills and develop cognitively and psychologically in similar ways.

From birth to approximately 6 months of age, infants display interest in the world around them, and have a desire to engage socially with the significant people in their lives. They begin to smile, babble, and coo at their parents, yearning for interaction with them. Language is still far from being mastered, but some children may say a few, simple words at this time. They are working hard to gain mobility by crawling or scooting and are also developing other large motor skills. Finally, trust begins to form as the baby's needs are met (or not met) by the caregiver, setting the stage for the Parent-Child relationship and attachment with the parent.

From 6 months of age to 1 year, a full range of emotions become visible and are communicated more clearly through behavior. As parents, we are able to tell if our child is sad, scared, angry, or surprised. The child still has few words that he can use to express himself, but other ways of communicating erupt at this time, such as clapping, belly laughs, and the shaking of the head to indicate "no" or "yes." During this time, children continue to try and engage with the people around them and are mostly focused on their primary caregiver. A fear of strangers may develop at this time, causing the baby to cling to his parents in new or unfamiliar situations. Lastly, attachment relationships are solidified during this time.

1 Year to 2 Years

Although physical development of children during this age range is not nearly as impressive as birth to 12 months, psychosocial development is fantastic! Language development at this time is also amazing, with children going from just a few simple words, to a large vocabulary. Some little ones will speak in short phrases, stringing words together to help their caregivers understand their wants and needs. The ability to walk and run are mastered, as well as climbing (on everything!), throwing, and even jumping can be seen during this time. The desire to explore the world is evident, but emotionally, our little ones still need us, their parents, to hold and cuddle them when the world becomes too overwhelming. Fearfulness of new people and situations continues to rise and peak during this time period. The early stages of empathy begin to develop, and the attachment the child has developed with his parents will now begin to affect the relationship he has with others. Finally, towards the end of this time period, children will begin to show the beginnings of temper tantrums, which are loathed and feared by ALL parents!

2 Years to 3 Years

As our young ones come into the second half of toddlerhood, emotions continue to develop as toddlers in this age group begin to evaluate themselves. Emotions such as empathy, embarrassment, and jealousy fully emerge, with the beginnings of guilt and shame taking root. We continue to see the fear of new situations and people throughout this time, and temper tantrums occur regularly as our toddlers begin to assert their will and become frustrated when they can't. Finally, language continues to explode with new word acquisitions occurring almost daily. They continue to string words together to form phrases, making it easier to understand their needs and wants. Some kids might even begin to speak in full sentences during this time.

6.2 Development in Early Childhood

Early childhood is a remarkable time. Your child's ability to communicate with you using words and appropriate body language fully comes into play by the end of early childhood. The Terrible Twos are gone, and there is peace in the home as your child becomes much easier to manage. The preschool years come and go, and the elementary school years step in. Your child becomes increasingly social with others, makes friends, and his personality is in full bloom, revealing to you a clear image of the person your child will become.

During early childhood, your child will make huge advances in understanding himself, as well as developing a deeper understanding of his emotions. With this understanding comes the ability to self-regulate, which is an important step towards controlling and managing difficult emotions, such as anger. Helping your child to understand their feelings during early childhood is an important step. Without teaching your child emotion regulation, you risk temper tantrums and anger outbursts as a common and regular occurrence in your household. Language fully develops during this time, with your child's speech being akin to that of an adult. Finally, your child's pattern of social interaction becomes more habitual, and as such, patterns of bullying behavior or victimization may become established at this time.

6.3 Development in Middle Childhood

In middle childhood, children become physically capable of anything! With improved balance, increased speed, and more control, children are highly active during this time. Running, jumping, climbing, and skipping, among other large motor skills, are fully developed. It's important to keep kids moving during this time, ensuring that they get plenty of physical exercise for overall health and well-being. Cognitively, children in middle childhood understand cause and effect, have the ability to consider multiple perspectives at one time, and multitasking becomes much easier to manage.

Emotion regulation is greatly improved during middle childhood, especially if caregivers have helped their child develop a good understanding of emotion and healthy coping skills to manage difficult feelings. The foundation built early on in the Parent-Child relationship helps to create harmony and mutual understanding between the child and the parent, setting the stage for the challenging years ahead in adolescence. Finally, towards the end of middle childhood, friendships become more intimate, and the opinions of friends begin to outweigh the opinions of caregivers.

6.4 Development in Adolescence

Adolescence is a trying time for parents. Puberty hits and, with it, a wave of physical and emotional changes. Sexuality develops with an increasing curiosity and desire to explore the opposite (or same) sex as the body becomes sexually mature for procreation (something no parent really wants to deal with). With puberty comes the wave of cliché mood swings that can leave parents feeling confused and exhausted. During this time, children are trying to discover who they are in comparison to their parents and their peers, and they are trying to determine where they belong in society. It's an awkward time.... As our teens try to discover their own personal identity, they also clash frequently with us, butting heads with their parents on an almost daily basis. This consistent bickering and "attitude-giving" is a sign of **individuation**, the natural process of gaining a sense of individuality (i.e. forming a separate identity from others, such as parents) (Amsel, *Individuation*). It is a normal struggle in gaining autonomy for teens and young adults (but a headache for us as parents!).

In many ways, adolescence mirrors toddlerhood where, in both cases, the child is caught between wanting to be free to do as he wishes but is also not quite ready to face the world alone. There is a teeter-tottering that occurs as the child struggles between wanting independence and needing parental support. Adolescence comes complete with temper tantrums too! Just replace throwing themselves on the floor with door slamming and stomping out of the room.

***

Although this chapter is not extensive in any way, this brief rundown of child psychosocial development should be enough of a foundation for us to work with as we discuss the Parent-Child relationship from birth to adulthood. For this chapter, you'll notice we don't have any specific exercises. As opposed to completing an exercise, I recommend checking out the following books and websites for additional reading to supplement this chapter. Find something that is specific to your child's developmental stage and dig in!

- *The Emotional Life of the Toddler* by Alicia F. Lieberman
- *Ages and Stages: A Parent's Guide to Normal Childhood Development* by Charles Schaefer and Theresa Foy DiGeronimo
- *Erik Erikson's Stages of Psychosocial Development* by Saul McLeod (simplypsychology.org)
- *Physical and Psychosocial Development Resources for Parents of Adolescents and Young Adults* by the Society for Adolescent Health and Medicine (adolescenthealth.org)
- *Signs of Normal Development Stages* by The Whole Child (thewholechild.org)

7

Understanding Emotions & Behavior in Children

Emotions are complex. They are a normal part of being human, and to be devoid of emotions is problematic. Emotions play a vital role in our safety, survival, and even help us in task accomplishment. Emotions are vital to human behavior and understanding the role emotions play in behavior is key to knowing how to manage difficult emotions in children.

In *AoP*, we discussed *Cognitive Behavioral Therapy* (CBT) and how this approach is used to create behavioral change. We reviewed how thoughts cause emotions which then trigger behavior:

Thought ⟶ Emotion/Feeling ⟶ Behavior/Action

Understanding how thoughts relate to emotions, which then trigger behaviors, lays the foundation for understanding our children's behaviors. From there, we need to understand what types of behaviors are elicited by different emotions. For the purposes of this chapter, I am going to boil emotions down to a basic few: joy, anger, fear, anxiety, and sadness. I think it could be argued that most emotions stem from these five. For example, jealousy, a very powerful emotion that can exist between siblings, could be considered a subset of "fear." Jealousy stems from insecurities of not being "good enough," of not being deserving of love, etc. These insecurities are essentially based in fear (i.e. "I'm afraid that I'm not *good enough*").

When we look at these five emotions, fear, anxiety, and anger tend to be the ones that produce the most problematic behaviors. Anxiety can be considered a subset of fear, but anxiety, as its own emotion, will play a bigger role in future chapters, so I want to make sure we have a firm understanding of this emotion on its own. We will be looking at "natural anxiety" in specific and understanding how it ties into the need for structure, discipline, and so on, in the home.

7.1 Anxiety & Fear

Anxiety is a complex emotion. Some people will use the term "nervous" to reflect this feeling. As mentioned previously, anxiety is a type of "fear" response in the body. You have the same physical response to anxiety as you do with fear. That is because these two emotions release the same stress hormone in your body, thereby producing the same effect, known as your "Fight or Flight" response.

So, what kind of behaviors are produced in children by fear and anxiety? All sorts of behaviors come to play, depending on the thought that triggered the emotion. You might have *secretive* behaviors, such as hiding objects, isolative behaviors, or even lying. You could see your child running away from situations (figuratively and literally) or crying. You might also get an anger response, such as tantruming (we'll talk more about this later in this chapter). These behavioral responses often result from **natural anxiety**.

Natural Anxiety in Children

I think we can all agree that children do not hold a place of power in any known society. Adults have that place, not children. Infants are at the mercy of their parents or caregivers, and are helpless for quite some time. In fact, most kids need adults to assist them in most things until the age of five or six, when they finally begin functioning more independently. That doesn't mean, however, that our children don't need our help past the age of six. I guarantee we all know at least one teenager who needs help every day with something! (*"Mom! I can't find my shoes!"* Sound familiar at all???) For all children, and especially young children, *natural anxiety* is what helps to keep them safe. It is the emotion that triggers them to be fearful of strangers, to stay close to mommy or daddy, and to be suspicious of possible poisons (*"Ewww! Is that a vegetable?!?"*). But how did this natural anxiety develop and why?

These questions are best answered when we consider an evolutionary perspective. All human beings are animals and mammals. Instead of talking about humans, let's talk about other mammals, such as zebras or lions. Most mammals are pack animals or travel in herds. There is typically a leader (usually male) and several females with their young. Young zebras typically stay very close to their mothers. They may play with others, but never far from their mothers. Why? They are prey animals, and have a normal, instinctual anxiety about predators. Wandering too far from the herd leaves them vulnerable to predators, such as lions. The same is true for lion cubs. Although they are predatory animals, they are still vulnerable to other predators, such as hyenas, and need their mother for protection. For both of these animals, the mother is also the source of food. To lose her means to lose their source of nutrition, and thus, guarantees their starvation and eventual death.

Finally, what about strangers? Both of these animals are led by male leaders. When a new male arrives, he must challenge the current leader, and the two must battle. If the newcomer wins, he takes over and will kill all the young. Mothers will do their best to protect their young, but often aren't able to. As such, "the stranger" signals impending doom for the babies. This is true for lions, zebras, and most mammals.

So, now that we've had a zoology lesson, what does this have to do with human beings? Well, human beings are considered mammals and, as such, it would make sense that our own young would still have very primitive emotional responses. As infants, we rely on instinct and instinct tells us to stay close to our caregivers. Just like in the animal world, our parents are our source of food, warmth, protection, and comfort. To be abandoned by them would ensure death. So, it is only natural that infants will develop anxiety surrounding the separation of their caregivers. As the child grows, the anxiety will change to match the new circumstances, such as anxiety about getting in trouble or fear of rejection. Just like we have evolved into more sophisticated creatures, so have our anxieties.

7.2   Sadness

No one wants to see their child in a sad mental state. As parents, we always want to see our children happy and healthy, but that isn't always the case. Sadness is a normal emotion that all human beings feel, and our children must learn to *feel* it and effectively cope with it too. Typically, it is an uncomfortable feeling for people to encounter and, unfortunately, in an effort to comfort others, many of us make matters worse by saying and/or doing the wrong thing. With children, it is no different. I have encountered many parents who shut down their children's emotions without realizing it. This is a topic all on its own, and we will cover this a little later in much more depth. For the purposes of this chapter, we want to look at how sadness affects behavior.

Sadness can develop into chronic conditions such as Persistent Depressive Disorder or Major Depression. In all cases, common behavior in sad or depressed children might be crying, isolating, poor sleep, low self-esteem, acting "needy," irritability/anger, and tantrums. Most people are surprised when they learn that sadness in children can be expressed as irritability and anger, and they are curious why this is. The reasoning goes back to the point made previously in this chapter, that children are not in a place of power. I think we can all agree that feeling "sad" leaves one feeling vulnerable. If you're a child, you are *already* vulnerable! To feel sad only deepens that sense of vulnerability, making you feel even more powerless in your life. As such, children would rather shift into a "stronger" emotion (typically anger), which feels less vulnerable and more powerful. It is important to note that this shift in emotion is a subconscious one and that it occurs so easily in children (and adults!) because anger is a "secondary" emotion.

7.3 Anger

Anger is a special emotion, and a complex one too. Something that I frequently teach my clients in therapy is that anger is a secondary emotion, typically caused by fear, hurt, or frustration, or some combination thereof. Think of it this way, anger is like a pot of water. The water cannot boil on its own; it needs a heating element. Imagine then, this pot of water on the stove with flames warming the water, slowly bringing it to a boil. In this analogy, you are the pot, the water is your level of anger, and the flames are the emotions: Fear, Frustration, and Hurt (i.e. Primary Emotions).

As you experience a primary emotion, such as frustration, you begin "heating" the anger inside you (i.e. the water). Eventually, these emotions can become too great, causing you to become overwhelmed, and thus, boil over (or having an anger outburst). This concept of "anger as a secondary emotion" can be hard to grasp, and I am often challenged by my clients in therapy on this one. In therapy, I usually give them examples of how each one of these emotions turn into anger. Let's look at an example:

Jim and his 5-year-old, Lilly, are at the park. Jim instructs Lilly to "stay where I can see you," and then goes to sit on a bench and check-out social media on his phone while Lilly plays. He continuously looks up to check on her, smiles and waves, and then goes back to his phone. After a few moments, he looks up and realizes that Lilly is no longer on the playground. Jim looks around, and when he realizes that she is nowhere to be seen, he gets up and begins searching the park. After several minutes, Jim's heart begins to race as he realizes he can't find Lilly. Suddenly, he is tapped on the shoulder behind him.

"Excuse me, is this your daughter?"

Jim turns to find Lilly, safe and sound. "Yes, thank you." As the stranger leaves, Jim raises his voice, firmly stating, "Lilly! Where were you! I told you to stay where I could see you! I thought something happened to you!"

"I'm sorry Daddy. Don't be mad, please! I was chasing a butterfly...."

Looking at this example, I think it is easy to see that Jim is angry with Lilly for not following directions. If we look deeper, however, we can see that Jim is not simply angry, he was scarred. When he realized he could not find his daughter, he feared the worst. We might also say that Jim felt frustrated with Lilly because she did not stay within his view. Hopefully, with this example, you can see how anger is really triggered by primary emotions.

Exercise: Reflect

Have you ever felt like Jim before? Was there ever a time that you were so fearful for the safety of your child that you actually felt angry with them? What happened? Why did you feel so scared? Why did you express your fear as anger? Take a moment to reflect on these questions. Write down any insights you gain from this reflection:

_____

_____

_____

_____

_____

Exercise: Connect

Think of the last time your child had a temper tantrum or anger outburst. If you have an infant, think of the last time they cried. What happened in that situation? What led to the outburst or crying spell? Write down just a few key events of this situation.

_____

_____

_____

_____

_____

_____

When infants cry, we often identify that our child is "sad" because they are crying. But toddlers and older children will cry when they are angry too. Why is that? It goes back to our previous boiling pot analogy. They cry because underneath that anger is hurt, frustration, and/or fear.

Thinking about the last time your child had an outburst (or a crying spell for infants), try to identify what the underlying emotion was for your child. Were they:

- Hurt?
- Scared?
- Frustrated?
- Some combination of the above?

If you're not sure, pick one, and then try to rationalize why your child would feel this way. For example:

My infant woke up in the middle of the night and began to cry. He cried for 15 minutes before I finally gave up and went to console him.

In this scenario, what underlying emotion might trigger this crying spell?

1. Hurt: The infant might be sad to find himself alone. He might feel sad by the fact that he has been left behind by his mother and she is nowhere to be found. (Remember, the infant doesn't understand that he is safe in his own room. All he knows is that he is alone without his parents.)

2. Fear: The infant is fearful for his safety because he is alone in the dark. Knowing that his parents are the key to his safety and survival, he cries for them. He knows that his parents, if they can hear him, will come to his rescue, and keep him safe.

3. Frustration: The infant is frustrated that he has been left alone again. He expects that his parents will stay near him because he trusts that they will keep him safe, but every night, after he falls asleep, they leave him alone. This gap between his expectation of what his parents will do and the reality of what his parents actually do produces this emotion of frustration.

4. Combination: We can imagine that frustration might be laced with any of the previously listed emotions.

Now it's your turn! Take the situation you briefly described for this exercise. Going through each emotion, try to put yourself in your child's shoes and rationalize why your child might have been feeling hurt, scared, or frustrated (no need to do the combination). Complete the sentence:

1. My child was angry because they were hurt. They were hurt because:

_____

_____

_____

2. My child was angry because they were scared. They were scared because:

_____

_____

_____

3. My child was angry because they were frustrated. They were frustrated because:

_____

_____

_____

What's it like to view your child's behavior and expression of anger in this way? Hopefully, having a deeper understanding of what is going on in your child's head gives you a better idea of how you might want to manage their anger in the future.

Exercise: Respond

Next time your child gets angry, try to take 5 minutes to reflect on what the underlying emotion is that your child is experiencing. Once you have a few ideas, bounce these ideas off with your child. Ask them if they are feeling hurt, scared, or frustrated. See what they tell you.

You might be surprised at the response you get! Once you try this out, write down some notes from the experience. Consider some of the following questions in your reflection:

- How did your child respond to being asked about hurt, fear, and frustration?
- Was your child able to acknowledge their underlying emotion easily or did they need your help?
- Did you find yourself feeling more empathetic once your child was able to express their underlying emotion?
- How did the situation end? Better than before? Worse than before? Why do you think it was better or worse?

_____

_____

_____

_____

_____

_____

_____

_____

_____

***

Now that we've come to understand the basic emotions of children and have connected some of the typical behaviors you will see, it's time to move forward. In the next chapter, we are going to continue our conversation about emotions. We'll take a look at emotion regulation, distress/frustration tolerance, and review ways you can help your child build these vital skills.

8

Emotion Regulation

Emotion regulation is the way a person controls and/or regulates the emotion they are experiencing at any given time. In *AoP*, we used the analogy of a stove to better understand this concept. Young children (such as toddlers) and older children (such as those in puberty) tend to have poor emotion regulation. In many ways, emotion regulation is attached to emotional maturity, but other factors, such as personality and temperament, also play a role.

When I work with children who have poor emotion regulation, the two key components to helping them are:

1. Assisting the child in understanding the emotion they are experiencing at any given time

2. Helping them develop ways to cope and calm themselves down when upset

The first part is important because, in order to help prevent anger outbursts or temper tantrums, a child must first be able to tell that they are reaching their point where their pot will boil over. Understanding their emotions, how their emotions play out in their body, as well as being able to label and identify their emotions, goes a great distance in helping children learn how to calm themselves down when upset. The second component, which is the actual act of helping them calm down, is related to teaching them coping skills or behaviors that they can engage in that help them to de-escalate their own emotional response.

In *AoP*, we discussed where emotion regulation comes from, diving deep into the concepts of temperament, personality, and **modeling**. All 3 of these are important to understand as a parent. For the purposes of this book, we won't be going into these 3 topics. There are definitions located in the glossary to help refresh your memory of this topic, and, of course, you can always review *AoP* for more information.

8.1 Poor Emotion Regulation

In order to better understand where you want to go with a child's emotion regulation, you must first understand where your child is at. As such, I'm going to help you better understand what would be considered poor emotion regulation in children.

With young children, temper tantrums are commonly witnessed as poor emotion regulation. Temper tantrums can also be considered normal human development for young children between the ages of 18 months and approximately 3 ½ years old. This time is frequently known as the "Terrible Two's," but can often persist a little after the age of 2. But what is considered a temper tantrum? In my experience, the definition of a "temper tantrum" changes from family to family. I have seen parents label a child crying because they are upset a "temper tantrum," and I have seen parents label a child who has thrown himself on the ground as having a "temper tantrum."

Alicia Lieberman describes a temper tantrum as an individual throwing themselves on the floor while crying and screaming in anger (61). For myself, I like to define a **temper tantrum** as an emotional reaction that is beyond what would be considered "normal" for that particular event. For example, a 10-year-old child who is told they need to wait one minute while a parent finishes a task before they can start a new activity may very well become upset, frown, and talk back. This, although annoying, is not necessarily a temper tantrum because it is not a reaction that is "beyond" what would be considered "normal" given the child's age and developmental level. Now, if in this same scenario the child were to throw themselves on the ground and begin screaming and kicking, that would be considered a temper tantrum because the reaction is beyond what would be considered "normal." The reason why the second is considered a temper tantrum as opposed to the first is because, in the first, the child is merely displaying displeasure with the response received from their parent. It is important to remember that our children are allowed to feel anger and to be upset when they are not getting what they want. In the second scenario, the reaction seems a bit much for a child who was told to just wait a minute. Typically, most mental health professionals will consider a tantrum to consist of a child who throws himself on the floor, kicks, screams, hits, and cries uncontrollably for a period of time that seems out of the ordinary.

Now, many parents want to know where temper tantrums come from, why do they happen, and how can they prevent them. As I have stated previously, I truly believe that you must know where you are coming from in order to know where you have to go. In my experience working with child behavior, this notion is absolutely true. A huge component of changing behavior comes from understanding why your child is engaging in that behavior to begin with. What purpose does the behavior serve for your child?

There are three primary reasons why a child will engage in tantrum-like behavior. For your child, the reason may be one or any combination of these. We will discuss each one individually in order to gain a deeper understanding of the problem at hand. It is also important to note that, although I am talking about temper tantrums, which can be considered typical behavior for young children, these reasons that we are about to discuss can be just as true for teens or older children who engage in anger outbursts.

Lack of Ability to Communicate

I think we can all agree that young children typically lack a full and varying vocabulary. Although they may be able to get general points across to people, they still lack enough sophistication and a broad enough vocabulary to really express themselves. Because the child can't effectively communicate their inner experience, they become frustrated. If we remember back in our previous chapters on anger and emotions, I mentioned that anger is a secondary emotion fueled by frustration, hurt, fear, or some combination of these. In this situation, when a child has difficulty expressing him or herself, they become frustrated because they cannot vocalize and express their frustration in a way that caregivers are able to adequately understand and address. This then results in tantruming behavior. Furthermore, this frustration also comes with feelings of being misunderstood. It's easy to see that, if a child can't explain exactly what it is that they need or want from a caregiver, and a caregiver is left to guessing and trying to decipher what it is that the child is trying to say, the child will feel misunderstood by the caregiver and, thus, lead to increased frustration and eventually some sort of anger outburst.

Teens frequently feel misunderstood and, as a result, will oftentimes shut their emotions in (i.e. internalize emotion), and will not speak to their parents about what it is they are internally experiencing. Instead, they tend to speak more to friends, feeling that their friends have a better ability to understand them and their internal emotional experience. This buildup of internal emotion, however, can create a volcanic effect where too much pressure builds within the teen, and they explode in an outburst of emotion. At times, this explosion of emotion may be witnessed as crying spells but is more frequently witnessed as an anger outburst.

Exercise: Connect

Do you think that poor communication could be partially responsible for your child's misbehavior? If you're not sure how to answer that question, consider these next questions first:

Is your child a baby, toddler, or adolescent?

Yes   No

Does your child suffer from a speech impediment, autism, or another developmental and/or cognitive delay?

Yes   No

When your child is angry, are they clearly able to express to you what emotion they are feeling and 'why'?

Yes   No

Does your child frequently feel exasperated when trying to explain things to you?

Yes   No

Does your child frequently give up trying to explain things to you?

Yes   No

Does your child rarely talk to you about what is bothering them?

Yes   No

Now, based off of your answers, consider this question again:

Do you think that poor communication could be partially responsible for your child's misbehavior?

Yes   No

If you marked "yes" to several of the previous questions in this exercise, then you can be sure there is a communication problem that needs to be addressed if you want to see things turn around for the better.

Poor Modeling

One of the more consistent themes of this book is the importance of good modeling coming from parents to their children. When it comes to emotion regulation, this is no different. Frequently in therapy, I have treated children who engage in temper tantrums or anger outbursts, but the child isn't the only one in the family doing these things. The parent is also guilty of these behaviors.

Exercise: Reflect

Take a second to reflect on yourself and try to be as honest with yourself as you can. Consider the following questions:

- Do you ever storm out of a room when upset?
- Have you ever run out of the house to take a walk when angry?
- Do you ever yell at your partner in heated arguments?
- Have you ever caught yourself making statements such as, "He's such an idiot," "I don't know why I'm with him," or "I should leave... these people are stupid"?
- Have you ever engaged in name-calling towards your partner, or perhaps the co-worker who has upset you?
- Have you ever insulted others on purpose during an argument (even if you really don't mean what you're saying)?

- Have other people called you "dramatic" or "emotional" before?
- Are others often telling you to "calm down" or "chill out"?

If you can identify with several of these, then there's a chance that you're modeling poor emotion regulation to your child. This can make us defensive... don't be. Many of us struggle with poor emotion regulation. And the first step to solving any problem is to acknowledge and recognize that it is even there! Another thing to keep in mind is that most parents are guilty of these behaviors during periods of high stress, which would include anger.

Now, if you responded "no" to all of these questions, then good for you! I would challenge you, however, to ask a family member or a friend whom you trust if you engage in any of the behaviors above. Let that person give you an objective opinion on how you act during times of high stress. You may be surprised to find that you are also guilty of tantrum-like behavior.

It is important to be able to identify what behaviors we, as parents, are also engaging in that might be influencing our children and showing them that such behaviors are appropriate during periods of high stress. No one is perfect, but identifying these common mistakes allows you to become more aware of yourself. This helps you to develop a game plan on what you need to do in order to be a better example for your children.

Parents are not always to blame for poor modeling. Older siblings and family friends with whom children spend a large amount of time with, grandparents who watch your children after school, or peers can be a poor influence on your children and their behavior. If you know that you are not guilty of engaging in tantrum-like behavior, then you may want to take a second to evaluate who are the significant people in your child's life whom they spend a lot of time with. How do those people respond during fits of anger or high stress? If these individuals do not seem to be the problem, it might be time to start looking at your child's friends and determining if these peers are appropriate social companions for them.

Temperament

Temperament can be defined as an individual's typical way of responding to the world and others (Santrock 136). It is your base from which you act and react. Some folks have a very mild, easy going personality and/or temperament, whereas other people may be a bit more spirited and intense in the way they act and react to situations. Temperament is going to play a big role in how you act under times of stress, and it is no different for your child. Researchers have worked hard to define and classify temperament. Although there are a few different classifications for temperament, the most well-known are the ones suggested by Alexander Chess and Stella Thomas. They identified 3 basic temperament styles:

1. **Easy Child**- Children with this temperament are generally happy and positive children. They adapt to changes in their lives without too much trouble, adopt new experiences with ease, and quickly settle into new routines as infants.

2. **Difficult Child**- A child that would fall into this category is a little more difficult (as the name implies). Children in this category cry frequently, struggle with changes in their lives, and tend to react negatively. Their moods can be intense. Children who fall into this category are more prone to temper tantrums and/or anger outbursts.

3. **Slow-to-Warm-Up Child**- Children with this temperament are typically seen as "low energy." They can be somewhat negative, struggle to adopt changes to their lives or daily routine and have mild moods.

There is little you can do to change a child's temperament, but you can help teach your child ways to manage their temperament during times of anger and stress. This goes along with teaching your child how to regulate themselves during these situations. This is going to be a big focus of this chapter later on.

Exercise: Connect

Take a moment to reread the 3 temperament styles. After reading, consider each one and determine which one most greatly describes your child. If you have more than one child, repeat this exercise for all your children. Write down the name of your child and the temperament you identified for them.

_____

_____

_____

_____

_____

_____

8.2 Older Children and Teens

We've discussed young children and those pesky temper tantrums that have most parents feeling overwhelmed when it comes to raising toddlers. Now the time has come to discuss older kids and their infamous anger outbursts. My guess is, you won't be surprised to hear that anger outbursts are nothing other than "big kid" temper tantrums. They can feel more intense, but that is only because they are coming from older children. Since older children have better vocabulary, anger outbursts may consist of more verbal threats, hateful language, or making statements that are intended to hurt your feelings. In the end, however, this is no different than your toddler screaming at the top of their lungs because they couldn't have another cookie.

For older children, anger outbursts are caused for the same reasons as temper tantrums, but there are a few differences. The main difference is that, unlike toddlers, teens have a full range of vocabulary and a deeper understanding of emotions. At this point, your child should have also developed some coping skills that they can use to regulate themselves under times of stress. This doesn't mean that your child is immune to anger outbursts, but there should be fewer anger outbursts in a situation such as this. As a therapist, I've worked with many older children who fail to learn adequate coping skills, or perhaps they were taught that screaming and yelling were an appropriate way to manage anger via modeling from the important caregivers in their lives. In these situations, you may find your older child engaging in anger outbursts. Similar to young children, teens often feel misunderstood, which then produces frustration that causes anger. Teens frequently feel as though no one is listening to them, or that their opinion, thoughts, and feelings are not important. This leads to hurt, frustration, and fear, which causes that pot of anger to over boil.

Some teens don't engage in anger outbursts but, rather, engage in other risky behaviors to help regulate their emotions. Some of these behaviors might be running away from home, engaging in non-suicidal self-harm (such as cutting behaviors or picking at the skin), or they may have suicidal thoughts. All of these are a prime example of a child who is struggling to regulate their emotions and is seeking a way to discharge all of that pent-up energy, such as fear and hurt. This, in turn, helps them to feel more emotionally balanced.

In the sections to follow in this chapter, we will be discussing the nervous system and how some emotions, such as anxiety, can cause a fight or flight response in the body, which then gets stuck and needs to be discharged via a healthy coping mechanism. Towards the end of the chapter, we will discuss ways to teach your child developmentally appropriate coping skills that they can use to help regulate their emotions during times of stress.

8.3 Healthy Emotion Regulation

For the past 2 decades, there have been changes in how mental health professionals view trauma. Without going into the biology of it all, the basics are that the nervous system reacts to external stressors with the **Fight or Flight Response**.

Essentially, whenever you encounter a situation that your brain interprets as potentially threatening, your brain signals the body to engage in a Fight or Flight response. This causes a chain reaction that prepares your body to either fight for your life or run for your life. Now, your brain doesn't always interpret situations accurately. The part of your brain that is assessing potential life or death situations is a fairly primitive part and it doesn't interpret "gray areas" very well. It is very black and white. An example might be a fight with a spouse.

During a fight with your spouse, your brain is going to interpret the situation as a "dangerous" one. This, in turn, is going to trigger that Fight or Flight response. This is why you'll feel that surge of energy (i.e. adrenaline) or you might feel your heart pounding or stomach churning. These are all normal, bodily reactions caused by the Fight or Flight response. I think we can all agree that a fight with your spouse isn't a life or death situation (unless you are in a Domestic Violence relationship), but your brain doesn't see that this situation is a "gray area." Your brain just recognizes that this situation is a high intensity situation and that you are at a potential risk. In turn, your body kicks in with the Fight or Flight response.

Without going too much into the neuroscience and physiology, let's chat a bit about this response. The Fight or Flight response is also known as the **Stress Response**. In your brain, there's a part known as the amygdala. This part of the brain is located toward the base of the brain by the brain stem, and it governs your Autonomic Nervous System. This system has 2 branches, the Sympathetic and Parasympathetic branches. The Sympathetic branch is responsible for this stress response. The Parasympathetic is responsible for your **Relaxation Re-**

sponse. When your Sympathetic branch is activated, you go into a Fight or Flight response. When you calm down from the stressor, your relaxation response has been activated. I like to think of it as engaging your *PARA*chute, since the relaxation response is tied to the *PARA*sympathetic nervous system.

The most important thing to remember is that these 2 branches can't be activated at once. (Well, they can, but it's rare and not how the system is supposed to work.) Since both systems can't be activated at once, whenever you (or your child's) stress response is activated, the solution is ALWAYS to engage your parachute (i.e. activate your Parasympathetic branch). This can be done by using healthy coping skills and relaxation techniques, which we'll address later in this chapter. For more information on how this process works, consider doing some further reading[1]. For now, the important thing for you to understand is that we all have this survival mechanism in our bodies, and we all utilize this system automatically. This is a "survival" reflex and it can't be controlled. BUT... you can recognize it, learn to coach yourself through it, and develop skills that engage your parachute.

Now that you know about the stress and relaxation response, what does it have to do with emotion regulation? Well, when we go into a Fight or Flight response, we are functioning from that primitive place in our brain. We are not in great control of ourselves, and this is why we may say things or do things that we end up regretting later. Since we have this foundational knowledge, let's narrow the view a bit and look at how the stress response applies to our children.

I think we can all agree that when our children have temper tantrums or anger outbursts, they aren't regulating their emotions AT ALL! And you are accurate in this thought process. When our children are in that headspace, they are not regulated, they are not thinking clearly, and they are very much in a Fight or Flight response. In fact, they are (what I like to call) *past their point of no return.*

The Point of No Return

Have you ever watched a movie where the main character comes up to a fork in the road? One of the paths leads to this bright and sunny looking trail and the other path leads to this dark and scary forest. And of course, the scary forest usually has some signs out that say *Beware, Turn Back,* or *Enter at Your Own Risk.* Can you picture that scene in your mind's eye? Hold that image for a moment, because we are going to need it.

When we find ourselves in situations where we are becoming emotional and reactive, our body usually gives us little signs that we are getting upset. This might be an increase in heart rate, ringing in your ears, heavy breathing, tingling in the arms or legs, etc. It's a little different for all of us, but we all have some of these bodily signs that we are starting to get angry. This is the fork in the road. When you start sensing all of these bodily signs, these are your *warning* signs. They are the *Beware* and *Turn Back* signs that your body is screaming at you, letting you know that you are starting to go down into the scary forest of emotional meltdown!

Exercise: Reflect

Take a moment and think about your warning signs. We all have them, but sometimes we lack awareness to what these signs are. For myself, I experience my heartrate increase and I'll get a shot of warmth that strikes in the center of my chest and then expands outwards. What about you? What do you notice happens to your body when you are becoming angry?

_____

_____

_____

_____

_____

_____

_____

_____

If you ignore these warning signs and choose to continue down the same path, you will approach your *Point of No Return*. This is the point in the story where the main character has gone down the path of the scary forest, and he's too deep into the forest to turn around. Perhaps he goes into the forest and then tries to turn back but realizes he's lost. Or maybe he's in the forest and the villain has circled behind him, blocking his path of escape. Whatever the reason, the hero of the story is now stuck in the forest, and the only way out is to continue forward. This is the *Point of No Return*, where there *is* no turning back.

When you ignore your body's warning signs, and you keep going down the scary forest path, you eventually come to a point where there is no turning back. Your emotions have become too great and your primitive brain (sometimes referred to as the Reptilian Brain) has taken over. You are fully engaged in your Fight or Flight response. That's it... game over! You've gone past the *Point of No Return*. For your child, this is their temper tantrum, their anger outburst, etc.

Exercise: Connect

Now that you've identified your own warning signs, let's try and identify the warning signs your child gives you. What warning signs does your child give before they have an anger outburst? Here are some examples:

- Clenching fists
- Gritting teeth

- Narrowed eyes
- Foot stomping
- Pursed lips
- Shaking their head
- Looking down at the floor
- Frowning
- Exasperated sighs
- Rapid breathing

These are just some examples of outer signs. There's a whole lot happening inside their bodies that you can't see, like accelerated heartrate, but there's a lot happening on the outside too! These are the signs you need to be looking for. These signs help you know when an intervention needs to be applied in order to help your child regulate their emotions. What outer signs does your child give you?

_____

_____

_____

_____

_____

_____

_____

Hopefully that analogy of the scary forest helps you to understand what happens to you when you lose your "cool" as a parent, but also what happens to your child when they have a meltdown. Essentially, this lack of emotional control is the result of a Fight or Flight response. For some individuals, their Fight or Flight response is triggered very easily and quickly. This is usually an individual who has a low **frustration tolerance** (also known as *distress tolerance*). For individuals whose Fight or Flight response is *not* easily triggered, they have a high frustration tolerance.

Elaine Miller-Karas is the author of *Building Resilience to Trauma: The Trauma and Community Resiliency Models*, and in her book, she discusses the **Resilient Zone**. In Elaine's model, this emotional meltdown is when a person has been bumped out of their Resilient Zone. Now, her book goes on to talk about how being bumped out of the Resilient Zone leads to trauma. We're not going to go down that road of discussing trauma because that's a whole book in itself and it deviates from the purpose of this book, which is to help you understand the basic mechanisms of successful parenting. What's important for you to understand right now is that we all have a Resilient Zone. In order to understand the concept of the Resilient Zone, let's use an analogy, which I like to refer to as your *Emotional Cup*.

Your Emotional Cup

Imagine that you have a cup, and this cup is your capacity to tolerate stress. Whenever you encounter a stressful event, water is poured into this cup. The more stressful the event, the more water is poured in. The longer the stressful event lasts, the more water is poured in. As such, we can see that the magnitude of a stressful event, as well as its chronicity (meaning how long the stressor is happening for), the more water is placed into your cup. The problem with this is that we all have a limit. Our cup can only take so much fluid before the water overflows and spills out everywhere. This is equivalent to being bumped out of our Resilient Zone or going past our point of no return.

In *AoP*, we reviewed the need to empty out this cup in a calm and controlled fashion in order to avoid your cup overflowing (i.e. an emotional meltdown). The key was engaging in self-care and utilizing healthy coping skills. By doing this, you empty the water out of your Emotional Cup in a controlled way. This allows you to stay in control of your emotions and actions. When you are in control of your emotions and actions, you are functioning within your Resilient Zone. This means that you have not come to that fork in the road that leads to the scary forest OR you have chosen to take the bright and sunny path, effectively avoiding the scary forest.

Some of us are born with a better capacity to handle stress, and some of us are born with a much smaller capacity, but this doesn't mean we are doomed to constantly being overwhelmed by life and always overflowing! You have the ability to empty your cup out regularly in a controlled manner with good self-care.

Now, just like you have an Emotional Cup, so does your child, and children (by their very nature) are more likely to have their cup overflow much more easily than adults. This is because children have low frustration tolerance and lack the skills needed to empty out their cup in a controlled way. This is where the parenting part comes in. As the parent, your job is to help your child learn ways to empty their cup in a controlled way. You may do this through:

- Modeling healthy coping skills
- Teaching your child coping skills
- Helping them engage in regular self-care activities

With that said, let's look further into what healthy coping skills are and how to do them so that you can begin emptying your own cup AND help your child empty their cup too!

8.4 Healthy Coping Skills

Let's shift gears and begin looking at what coping skills are. I think this term sounds elusive. It leaves people wondering how you gain coping skills and utilize them effectively. We're going to break this whole thing down into 2 parts:

1. Defining coping skills and explaining how you use them
2. Provide a list of potential coping skills with directions for their use

By the end of this chapter, you'll gain some new skills for yourself and your child!

What are Coping Skills & How Do You Use Them?

Coping skills are different actions an individual can take in order to help them manage difficult emotions such as anger, anxiety, or sadness. Coping skills can help a person weather stressful life events to help minimize the psychological negative impact that the stressor may have on the individual. Using coping skills on a regular basis will help you empty your cup in a controlled manner when used frequently throughout the day or week. Using coping skills will also help to keep you from getting to your *Point of No Return* when you use them during a high stress situation. This brings us to the topic of how do you best use coping skills to make them most effective? It comes down to 3 tips:

1. Use them regularly
2. Apply them before your cup is too full
3. Layer them during high-stress situations.

For this workbook, we're going to dig into each tip a little more deeply, and of course, you'll have some exercises to try out to make you more effective at emptying your Emotional Cup.

Using Coping Skills Regularly

The biggest mistake I see clients make when trying to use coping skills is that they only use them when they are already upset. Doing this is setting you up for failure. Here's the secret to using coping skills *effectively*: You have to use them regularly when you are *not* upset! This may seem counter-intuitive, but it's the truth nonetheless.

Without going too far into the weeds with this topic, let me explain why using a coping skill regularly makes it more effective. Some coping skills, such as deep breathing, will force your body to slow down when used correctly. This helps to combat the *Fight or Flight* response. By practicing regularly, your brain forms an association with the skill as being soothing. It's the same concept behind bedtime routines.

Brain associations are common with many things we do. Our brain is biologically wired to form all of these connections in order to make life easier for us. In short, our brain LOVES routine and structure. The more structure and routine we have in our lives, the safer and more in control we feel in our life, producing a deep sense of security. That's what our kids love too!

When you begin practicing your coping skills on a regular basis during a calm and relaxed state, you help your brain to form an association between that skill and feeling relaxed. That association gets stronger and more powerful every time you do it because it strengthens those neural pathways in the brain. This means that when things get really tough suddenly, and you need your coping skills to help you calm down, it's going to be much more effective! Why? Because, not only are you engaging in a technique that is forcibly helping your body to slow down, but you've harnessed the power of brain associations to boost the calming effect that skill has on your emotions!

Practicing your coping skills regularly is going to have a dual effect in that, not only will you be forming that brain association, but you will also be emptying your *Emotional Cup* on a regular basis. Engaging in this practice means that you will feel overwhelmed less often and have a higher tolerance for stress and frustration. Don't be shocked if you encounter other beneficial effects too, such as lowered blood pressure!

Exercise: Reflect

What are your coping skills? Have you ever taken a moment to figure out what they are? What do you do to help yourself calm down? Consider some of these common ones:

- Take deep breaths
- Go for a walk
- Call a friend to vent
- Write in a journal
- Pray

These are examples of common, healthy skills. There are many maladaptive coping skills out there too. Consider some of these, and don't be afraid to admit to yourself if you engage in these to calm down:

- Using drugs
- Drinking alcohol
- Self-harm (like cutting or burning the skin)
- Destroying things (like breaking a glass or plate)
- Purposefully engaging in vindictive behavior

Take a moment to reflect on what *your* common coping skills are and write them down. It doesn't matter at this time if the skill is a healthy one or maladaptive. This is just supposed to be a moment of honest reflection with yourself.

_____

_____

_____

_____

_____

_____

Now that you have written down your coping skills, what coping skills does your child currently have and use? If you have an infant, they don't really have a coping skill, so you can indicate that. If you have a teen, then they definitely have some set of skills, but they may be a mix of healthy and maladaptive. Write them all down. The point of the exercise is for you to really reflect on what your child has RIGHT NOW as a coping skill that they engage in. If you don't know, that's ok too. Be honest with yourself and only include those skills you know they have because you have seen them actively engage in this skill.

_____

_____

_____

_____

_____

_____

Exercise: Connect

For this exercise, I want you to take the opportunity and look over your coping skills and the coping skills of your child in the previous exercise. If you have an infant, no need to do this exercise because it won't apply to you, but I recommend you still read through it since I'm going to share some valuable information. Now, after reviewing your coping skills and your child's skills, reflect on the following questions and write down any insights you obtain:

- Are any of the skills similar?
- Which ones are different?
- How did you learn to use the skills you have during stressful times?
- How do you think your child learned their coping skills? Who taught them?

_____

_____

_____

_____

_____

_____

_____

_____

_____

If you have a similar experience to most families, you may have noticed some similarities between your child's coping skills and your own. Many families notice generational patterns. For example, it is common for someone who uses alcohol to decompress at the end of the day to have parents who did the same thing, as well as grandparents, and even great grandparents. Similarly, if someone has a tendency to talk out their problems and vent, their children often share a similar way of managing their own problems, by venting to friends or their siblings. Kids who have parents that tend to be "yellers," are often "yellers" themselves, and so on.

This follows the idea of **social learning**. This theory was largely developed by Albert Bandura, a famous American psychologist. He believed that people learn different behaviors by watching and mimicking others (Papalia and Feldman, 31). Remember earlier in this chapter, we talked about "modeling"? Well, here it is in action!

Kids are human mirrors! They learn through observation and oftentimes reflect back what they see. One of the easiest ways to witness this is in coping skills. Usually, kids will share similar coping skills as their parents. Did you see that in this exercise at all?

Now, it's important to note that parents aren't the only ones our children are "socially learning" from. Family, friends, teachers, neighbors, and so on, are also playing a role in teaching your children how to cope with distress. But, as parents, you get first crack at this! So, make sure you're modeling something worth learning!

Using Coping Skills Before Your Cup Overflows

Sometimes, even though you've been practicing your coping skills every day, you still might find yourself overwhelmed. This is because the stressors you are encountering in your life are filling your cup faster than your daily routine is helping to empty it. It might also be because the stressor is a HUGE one, like a sudden death or traumatic event. In these situations, you need to begin applying your coping skills immediately.

I mentioned earlier in this chapter that your body gives off little warning signs to let you know that you are approaching your *Point of No Return*. This is the point where your cup is almost filled to the brim but isn't overflowing yet. Learning to recognize what those signs are is a key step in mastering stressful emotions. We all have these little warning signs. For me, I usually feel the turning of my stomach, like butterflies swirling around, which is then followed by a shot of adrenaline that I sense in my chest first (like a shot of warmth spreading outward from the center of my chest). When I sense these bodily signals, I know my body is preparing for a Fight or Flight response, which means my cup is filling up and I am approaching my *Point of No Return*. When I feel these sensations, I know it's time to start applying my coping skills. The same goes for you and your child!

Exercise: Reflect

Do you know what your warning signs are? The time has come to understand yourself a little deeper. Below are a list of common bodily signs of anger and distress. Circle all the ones that apply to you. Remember, you're looking for the ones that happen BEFORE you reach your *Point of No Return.*

Gritting Teeth   Clenched Fists   Accelerated Heartbeat

Nausea   Shallow Breathing   Tingling Sensations   Chills

Pursed Lips   Sweating   Warm Sensations   Numbing

Ringing in Ears   Dizziness   Muscle Tension   Headaches

Itchiness   Shakiness   Pacing   Pulling Hair   Tapping

Clicking the Tongue   Paralysis   Hot Flashes   Sighing

Rigidity   Accelerated Movements   Slowed Movements

Others not listed:

_____

_____

Hopefully, you were able to identify at least a few. Next time you start to feel angry, try to notice what is going on with your body. Learn how your body is trying to tell you that you are approaching your *Point of No Return.* Then, you'll be able to begin applying coping skills immediately so that your cup doesn't overflow! And to top it off, you'll be modeling to your child healthy emotion regulation!

Exercise: Respond

As for your child, do you know what their bodily signs are? Take a second to think on that for a moment. Next time your child starts to become dysregulated, try to catch what signs they are giving you that their cup is getting too full. If you have an older child, find a quiet time to sit with them this week and ask them directly. The more they understand their own body and emotions, the better for everyone! Here's that list again. This time, circle the bodily signs you've noticed for your child OR signs that your child reports to you.

Gritting Teeth   Clenched Fists   Accelerated Heartbeat

Nausea   Shallow Breathing   Tingling Sensations   Chills

Pursed Lips   Sweating   Warm Sensations   Numbing

Ringing in Ears   Dizziness   Muscle Tension   Headaches

Itchiness   Shakiness   Pacing   Pulling Hair   Tapping

Clicking the Tongue   Paralysis   Hot Flashes   Sighing

Rigidity   Accelerated Movements   Slowed Movements

Others not listed:

_____

_____

Start training your child to use their coping skills when they feel the symptoms they've endorsed above. Prompt your child when you notice them becoming distressed to use their skills. If needed, model those skills to them by doing it with them. Making an effort to practice these things will help keep your child from boiling over into a rage or deep depression and is key to building a resilient child.

Layer Coping Skills during Stressful Times

Sometimes, the stressor we are encountering is just too great. You might be engaging in your technique, but it doesn't seem to be calming you down enough. When this happens, individuals will give up. No single coping skill is so powerful that it can bring instant, lasting emotional relief during a high stress event. In situations like these, the secret is to layer different coping skills until you have regained control of yourself.

Let's look at this a little differently while considering a stressful emotion, such as anger, on a scale from 1 to 10. Ten is when the Emotional Cup has overflowed, and you are past your *Point of No Return*. A 7 or 8 on this scale might be when you begin to see your warning signs. A 5 or 6 is where you might feel emotional distress and you know you are getting angry, but your body isn't starting to kick in that Fight-or-Flight response yet. You are still level-headed enough to make good decisions and assess the consequences of your behavior. The numbers 1 through 4 on this scale represent differing levels of stress, but all minor enough that they are easily controlled. The situation might be considered nothing more than an annoyance or frustrating barrier.

If you are experiencing stress on that 1-4 scale, a coping skill might not even be necessary to use but can be effective in reducing the stress.

Once you reach 5-7, you should begin applying your coping skills, and you should find that they are helping you in reducing your rating or at least maintaining it so that your cup doesn't overflow. As you approach 7 - 9, you'll find that one coping skill will rarely do the trick. It's fairly ineffective, and this, in turn, will leave you discouraged. In this situation, you should begin using multiple skills to help maintain and reduce your stress.

For example, say you are at a 9, so you begin with a Deep Breathing technique. This brings you down to an 8, which isn't a huge improvement. So, you switch to Visualization which maintains you at an 8. Then you apply Grounding which brings you to a 7, and then you try Deep Breathing again which calms you further to a 6. This is called **Layering Coping Skills**, and it is very effective. It's not fast by any means, but it *does* work. The key is having a variety of coping skills that you have practiced over time to make them effective for you. Then, you must have enough discipline to apply those skills over and over again until you are back in control (around 4 or 5).

Layering coping skills is effective for multiple reasons:

- You are continuously forcing your body to calm down through relaxation techniques, which helps to stall out the *Fight or Flight*
- You are forcing your mind to shift its focus from the problem/ stressor to the coping skill, which helps to keep you from reigniting your *Fight or Flight*
- In general, the *Fight or Flight* response is a temporary, short-lived effect on the body, so layering coping skills helps you to regulate your emotions while riding out that response.

These 3 points are the *how* of coping skills. Many individuals have coping skills, but few use them correctly or appropriately. If you can begin mastering these 3 steps, you'll be more efficient at emptying your cup regularly. This will help you be a better parent because you'll be in more control of your emotions, less stressed, less burned out, and a lot less likely to yell all the time. Even more inspiring is that you'll be modeling these same skills to your kids! That means they'll start following your lead and using coping skills effectively to help themselves when they feel overwhelmed by emotion. Furthermore, because you'll be such an expert at it, you'll be able to coach them through it, which will benefit your Parent-Child Relationship. It's a total win-win for everyone!

Your Family's Coping Skills Toolkit

At this point, we've dived into a lot of different topics surrounding emotion regulation, but now we're going to learn some skills. I've already named a few in the section above, so you should have an idea of what coping skills look like. In this section, we are going to break down coping skills into two categories: Internal versus External coping skills.

1. **External Coping Skills** - Skills that fall in this category exist outside of you or require a physical object to work. For example, a stress ball is a well-known and classic stress relief tool. It's an external coping skill because it requires a physical object in order to work.

2. **Internal Coping Skills** - These are skills that don't require anything but you! Nothing else is required. Examples include Progressive Muscle Relaxation, Deep Breathing, Meditation, Visualization, Mindfulness, etc. Unlike external skills, internal ones utilize only your mind.

When I work with clients, I require that my clients master at least one external and two internal coping skills in treatment. There are good reasons why I require this. To begin, in order to layer coping skills in a high stress situation, you need multiple skills. In my work with intensely complex cases, 3 coping skills seems to be the minimum for effective emotion regulation. Mastery of more skills is even better, but 3 will get you by.

Another reason to have some external and some internal skills is because some work better than others in different situations. For example, if your child is in the middle of class taking a test, he may not be able to pull out a journal to reflect on his anxiety. In a situation like this, he must have an internal skill he can rely on. Similarly, in extremely high stress situations, like the sudden death of a family member, you may not have enough focus and self-discipline to practice a meditation. Your mind might be too overwhelmed already to make that internal coping skill function. In situations such as these, external coping skills are more effective, because they provide you with a tangible object that you can manipulate with your hands. This makes it easier to focus your awareness on something and get out of your negative headspace.

For the remainder of this chapter, we are going to build-up and create your family's Coping Skills Toolkit. For the following exercise, I recommend you complete the activities for yourself first, and then you'll repeat it with your child. This allows you to understand the whole concept and work out any "kinks" you might find in the process. Furthermore, completing this exercise for yourself will also help you develop your own resilience that you will then be able to model to your kids. Let's get started!

Exercise: Connect

Let's begin by looking at the answers to the *Reflect* exercise you completed earlier in this chapter (the one where you identified your coping skills). You should have made a list. Take a moment to practice identifying which one is an External Skill and which one is an Internal Skill. Remember, you are looking for a minimum of 3 skills (1 external and 2 internal). If you have more, that's even better! List the skills under the appropriate category:

External Coping Skill

_____

_____

_____

_____

_____

Internal Coping Skill

_____

_____

_____

_____

_____

How did you do? Do you have a combination of external and internal coping skills? If you do, you can move on to completing this exercise for your child. If you didn't have enough skills, it's time to learn some new ones.

Exercise: Respond

No matter how many skills you have, you can start working on your family's Coping Skills Toolkit. You can get as creative as you would like. This is a project you can do with your child, helping them make it for themselves. You can also create a shared, family toolkit where everyone in the family can contribute.

In the therapy room, my clients and I will build physical kits. This might be a shoebox, a recycled coffee can, etc. Most of my adult clients will use a recipe card box and a stack of index cards, but some families with young children enjoy the activity of decorating and hunting for objects. Here's what you'll need:

- A small container of your choice
- Small objects that fit in the container OR index cards
- Items to decorate with

The container is going to become your physical kit. The small objects will represent the different coping skills you, your child, and/or your family has. Allow your child to decorate the kit. Once completed, you should fill the kit with all the objects you have collected. If you can't find small objects, consider writing the coping skill on an index card and place that in the box. And voila! You have just created a Coping Skills Toolkit. So how do you use it?

As a therapist, I would spend countless therapy hours teaching my child clients different coping skills. But when the time came for my clients to use their skills, they would completely forget about them. I realized that my clients needed something tangible they could refer to to help them remember the skills they had learned. That's when I started creating Coping Skills Toolkits. Later on, I found the intervention helpful to families.

So, now that you have this kit, what do you do?

- **For Personal Use** – Remember how we talked about practicing your coping skills when you are already calm? You can use your kit to help! Create a daily ritual of practicing a coping skill. Pick a time of day (I usually recommend before bed to my clients) and set aside 5 to 10 minutes. Randomly select an object out of your kit and practice this skill. Repeat this practice daily. The other way to use this kit is to pull it out when you are overwhelmed and feel as though your Emotional Cup is too full. Take a 5 to 10 minute break, pull a skill out of the box, and begin practicing it. If you find that you are still upset, pull a second skill, and practice that one. Layer those skills until you feel as though you have regained control of yourself.

- **For Family Use** – Just like you used the kit to practice a coping skill daily, you can repeat the same exercise as a family unit. You can create a daily ritual where your family practices a skill together every day for 5 to 10 minutes. There are several advantages to this practice! Not only are you spending time with your child, but you are also modeling to them healthy coping skills! You are also getting them to practice a healthy coping skill on a regular basis, which will help your child regulate their emotions later on when they are upset. Like above, you can also use the Family Kit for your child when they are upset. If you notice your child is starting to approach their *Point of No Return*, it's time to direct them to pull a skill out of the kit. Have them practice the skill. If they need to, have them pull another one out. Once again, you are helping them remember to use their skills! The earlier you start this practice, the better and more effective it will be for your child.

Remember to always add more skills to your toolkit. The more you have, the better for you and your family!

[1] A simple article you can access online to learn more about the Fight or Flight Response is "health.harvard.edu/staying-healthy/understanding-the-stress-response"

9

A Wholistic Approach to Discipline

It has been quite the journey, and we are nowhere near being done yet! The time has come to tackle one of the most difficult topics, and that's discipline. Many parents aren't comfortable with discipline because it may bring up painful memories, they may not know how to do it, have limited knowledge of different disciplinary techniques (i.e. timeouts, spankings, removing privileges, etc.), or simply don't like doing it because it makes them feel badly. All of these things tend to give discipline a bad reputation.

By the end of this chapter, you will have a richer and fuller understanding of discipline. You'll be taking a much more wholistic approach that will empower you and give you fresh, invigorating ideas on how to manage your children. To begin, let's start with a new definition and understanding of discipline.

The word discipline comes from the root word *disciple*, which means "to teach." Therefore, **discipline** is the art of teaching our children. That's it! Pretty simple, right? Most people only see discipline as a punishment, but I am going to expand your way of thinking about discipline.

Wholistic Discipline (a component to my Wholistic Parenting approach) consists of love and affection, healthy boundaries, rules and limits, structure, praise, rewards, and consequences. A good disciplinarian has successfully mastered a balance between rewards and consequences, rigidity and flexibility. This is a wholistic approach to discipline. To understand this concept better, we will break it down further into its multiple parts. We will begin with the broader concept of the home environment and then hone it down to the parent-child relationship, which is your interaction with your child every day.

9.1 Home Environment

The home environment consists of three major components:

1. Structure & Routine
2. Rules & Limits
3. Rewards & Consequences

We are going to break down each one and take a closer look at how you can master these parts in your own household.

Structure & Routine

Most parents know that young children thrive on structure and routine. Alicia Lieberman, a child specialist, explained in her book that routines help to contain uncertainty and anxiety for children while providing them with reassurance (220). This, however, isn't just true for young children, it is also true for teens and adults. Human beings do best when they have knowledge about what to expect during different parts of the day. As adults, we feel more in control of our lives when we have some semblance of structure and routine. For children, a lack of structure and routine leads to feelings of insecurity and anxiety, which can produce defiant behaviors, emotional instability (i.e.

mood swings), and difficulty transitioning from one event to the next, among other struggles.

A well-balanced, structured home includes set times for work, play, sleep, and family time. Having a structured routine for your family does not mean you must be rigid in maintaining this routine. Flexibility is just as important as structure. It is okay to have flexibility in your daily schedule. The point of a structured home is to provide your child with some knowledge of what comes first, next, then after that. Let's look at an example....

Let's say the structure of dinnertime in your family is as follows:

- Saying grace
- Eating the main meal
- Eating dessert
- Cleaning the dinner table

On one day, you may follow this structure, and then the next day, you may need to clean the table first and have dessert afterwards. This is an example of a flexible routine where the family follows a general order of events, but the order is not set in stone. Another example may be one day you serve your child's lunch and then put him down for a nap. On the next day, you put him down for a nap first and *then* feed him lunch. The general routine is still in place where the child is having a nap around lunch time.

Having a routine doesn't mean that you must have a set schedule. You're just looking for a rough sketch of what your daily life looks like for you and your family. Some semblance of structure and routine throughout your day will greatly reduce the frequency and severity of temper tantrums, anger outbursts, and arguing about daily events in your household. Structure and routine help to accomplish this because your child will have less anxiety and feelings of insecurity because he knows what to expect throughout the day.

Exercise: Reflect

Does your family have a daily routine? Most families have some semblance of routine to their day. Take a second to think about what the average day looks like for you and your family. Consider that your weekly routine might differ from your weekend routine. Write down what your average daily routine looks like for your family.

_____

_____

_____

_____

_____

_____

_____

_____

_____

_____

Are you satisfied with this routine?

Yes   No

Does this routine meet your family's needs?

Yes   No

Does your routine need any adjustments to better serve you and your family?

Yes   No

Exercise: Connect

Has there ever been a time when your routine was disrupted? Going on vacation is a really good example of this. When you go on vacation, I'm willing to bet your day does not look like the routine you've just listed out in the previous exercise. Have you ever noticed what happens to your kids on vacation? Most kids display disturbed sleep patterns (i.e. struggling to fall asleep, tossing and turning, getting up much later or much earlier than normal, etc.), increased irritability or moodiness, are more argumentative, etc. Does this sound familiar?

What happens to your child when his or her routine is changed (such as vacation)? How does their sleeping patterns, eating patterns, attitudes, moods, and behaviors change when you take a family trip?

_____

_____

_____

_____

_____

_____

_____

_____

If your child doesn't change at all, consider yourself among the few! Most children experience some sort of change in behavior when their routine is adjusted. Maybe you've noticed these changes but just attribute the change to excitement or exhaustion from traveling, etc. Although these things certainly do contribute, it's not the only reason. The change in routine is actually playing a big role in your child's change in attitude and behavior. Infants and younger children are much more prone to these reactions when you switch up their routine. Older children have learned to regulate their emotions a little bit better, but they can still be prone to these problems.

Exercise: Respond

Ok, so you've written down your current daily routine and have done some reflection on how routines impact your child's behaviors. Now's the time to determine whether or not you like your family's routine. Does it meet your family's needs? Maybe you realized that you really don't have a routine at all, or perhaps that you have a routine, but it needs more structure. Whatever it is, take some time now to brainstorm how you would like your family's routine to look. Plan it out and write it down:

_____

_____

_____

_____

_____

_____

_____

_____

_____

_____

Now, here's the hard part: I want you to try implementing this routine for 2 weeks. Yup, 2 weeks! Just do the best you can. Expect your kids to push back a little and for their behaviors to become a little more unsavory. Remember, you're changing things on them, so they are going to react and push back! That's ok and completely normal. Just stick to the plan and follow your routine for 2 weeks. After 2 weeks, revisit this exercise and determine if something isn't working. See if you need to make any adjustments to make the routine more effective.

If you make adjustments, try the new routine out for another 2 weeks. Come back to this exercise and review the routine again. Keep doing this over and over until you find a routine you are satisfied with. Once you find a routine that is serving your family well, stick to it! Practice your finalized routine for 1 month. After a month, you should notice your kids settling into this new normal. They may still resist and push back a little bit but keep with it! After 2 months of practicing your finalized routine, everyone should be with the program and things should be running fairly smoothly.

Congratulations! You've just adopted and successfully implemented a family routine!

Rules & Limits

Your home environment should consist of appropriate rules and limits for your children. This includes developmentally appropriate consequences and rewards for different behaviors. The home environment should also consist of healthy boundaries and respect for all individuals in the home. This means that, not only should both parents show respect *towards* one another, but respect should also be demonstrated *towards* each child and *between* each child. Respect and healthy boundaries should be one of the cornerstone foundations to your home environment.

One of my first interventions with families is for parents to create a list of family rules. Then, I advocate for this list to be on display in the home. If you are like most parents (myself included), you've only thought of and enforced a family rule when the situation arose. For example, until your child told his first lie, you probably didn't even think of that as an established *family rule.* Sure, you knew that lying was going to be a *No-No* in your house, but you never actually thought of it, or considered what the consequences for lying would be, until your child told that first lie.

As parents, we are often flying by the seat of our pants, desperately trying to make it through another day. Parenting this way on a regular basis, however, will make it that much harder for you to be consistent in your parenting (something we will tackle a little later in this chapter). It also creates confusion, insecurity, and anxiety for your child because they don't understand what is being expected of them at any given time.

Having established family rules contributes to the structure of your home, and consequently, helps to teach your child how to function in society. The home environment should be a *microcosm* of the larger, outside world. One of our greatest tasks as parents is to prepare our kids to function in the society we have chosen to raise them in. Part of the reason why our society writes down laws is because it eliminates confusion and doubt. Your child's classroom has, without a doubt, a list of classroom rules and expectations. And these rules are probably on display for children to see every single day they walk into the classroom. There is wisdom in this practice, and your household should be no different.

Once again, your home should be a **microcosm**, a miniature version of the outside world. As such, having your "laws" (i.e. family rules) clearly written down and on display for all to see quickly helps to eliminate arguing, confusion and frustration. If your child knows exactly what is expected of him, then there is a higher likelihood that he will follow through with those expectations.

Exercise: Respond

Have you ever taken the time to actually write out your family's rules? If you have, you are ahead of the game. If you haven't, there's no time like the present! Find a quiet space where you can think clearly. If you have a co-parent, I recommend you collaborate with them on this exercise. You're going to list out the rules for your family. But here's the catch... these rules go for EVERYONE in the family, not just your child! That means that whatever you list on this page as a family rule, YOU are also subject to follow! Remember, kids are a mirror, and they reflect back your own behavior for the better or worse. As such, you must model the behavior you want to see in your kids. You have to "talk the talk" AND you must "walk the walk."

Your rules can be as broad or as specific as you want them to be. You can have as many or as few as you choose. So go ahead, and give it a shot! What are YOUR family's rules?

_____

_____

_____

_____

_____

_____

_____

Was that hard to do? Most parents find this exercise to be very taxing. Be proud of yourself for taking this task on. In the next section, we're going to take these rules to the next stage of development. For now, know that you can adjust these rules as needed. This should be a living document, meaning that you can add to them or adjust them as your family's needs, wants, and values grow. For now, your list is a great start!

Rewards & Consequences

This is a HUGE part of a Wholistic Discipline approach because Rewards & Consequences are at the heart of how you modify and shape your child's behaviors. Do you use Rewards & Consequences in your home? Most parents would answer *yes* to this question, but I'm going to challenge you and argue that you probably *don't*. I'm willing to bet that you *think* you do, but what you are actually engaging in is Bribery & Punishment.

Many parents come to me and share how they are disciplining their kids, thinking that they are engaging in giving rewards for wanted behavior and giving consequences for unwanted behavior. They soon learn from me, however, that what they've been doing all along is bribing their kids and punishing them. When this happens, the kids are actually the ones in control, not the parents.

As I mentioned previously, Rewards & Consequences play a major role in my Wholistic Parenting system. It is also a critical component to a structured, healthy, and loving home. The trick is all in HOW you administer the reward or consequence. It's a fine line, but the difference is made in the details.

Bribing vs Rewarding

If you were to google *bribe* you would get the following definition: "to persuade (someone) to act in one's favor, typically illegally or dishonestly, by a gift of money or other inducement" ("Bribe," def. 1). In this definition, we understand that we are trying to push, beg, and plead for someone to do something for us. Perhaps it is something that they would never do of their own volition. In this situation, the person receiving the bribe has control of the situation.

Let's compare this definition to that of *reward*. Googling this word would turn up the following: "a thing given in recognition of one's service, effort, or achievement" ("Reward," def. 1). In this definition, there is no begging, no pleading, no pushing for the other person to do what we want. The other person has done the work, and we are offering a prize for a job well done. In this situation, the person offering the reward has the control.

So how does this relate to parenting? I mentioned earlier that the difference lies in the details. To help explore this concept, I'm going to provide 2 examples:

Example 1

Mom: "Molly, please turn off your tablet. We have to get ready for school."

Molly ignores Mom and keeps playing.

Mom: Slightly more irritated, "Molly, turn off the tablet now. We are going to be late!"

Molly: "Ok Mom," she says, but continues to play on her tablet anyways.

Mom: "Molly, if you turn your tablet off right now, then I'll let you stay up 15 minutes later tonight."

Molly then proceeds to turn off her tablet.

Example 2

Mom: "Molly, please turn off your tablet. We have to get ready for school."

Molly ignores Mom and keeps playing.

Mom: Slightly more irritated, "Molly, when you turn off the tablet, then I can reward you for following directions."

Molly then proceeds to turn off her tablet.

Mom: "Thank you for listening to me and turning off the tablet. Since you listened to me, I'll allow you to stay up 15 minutes past your bedtime."

Take a moment to see if you can tell which example is "Bribing" and which example is "Rewarding." If you were able to do that, are you able to understand why? Let's start by identifying which one is the *bribe* and which one is the *reward*.

Example 1 is the *bribe*, which means Example 2 is the *reward*. But why? What are the details that make these examples different?

Closer Look at Example 1: The Bribe

Hopefully you can feel that Molly is the one in control of this situation from beginning to end. The primary issue is Mom's word choice. When it comes to *bribing* vs *rewarding*, those fine details have to do with semantics. Words have great power in parenting, and you're going to want to harness the power of words to your advantage!

In Example 1, Mom says:

"Molly, if you turn your tablet off right now, then I'll let you stay up 15 minutes later tonight."

She has engaged in an *If-Then* sentence structure that sets up the bribe. Think of other examples like this:

- "If you stop tantruming right now, then I'll give you a cookie."
- "If you behave for me in the store, then I'll buy you something."

- "If you do your homework, then I'll let you have dessert tonight."

Sometimes, bribes can be more obvious, usually because we are desperate:

- "Please stop screaming!! If you stop screaming, then I'll give you candy?!? What about a toy?!?"

When we bribe, the kid is in complete control of the situation. And, every time you bribe, you shift the power differential in your household. This means that the authority and power shifts from the parent to the child. (This was one of the fundamentals to our Parenting Philosophy in Chapter 1.) The more often you do this, the more often your child has the power. Overtime, if done frequently enough, that power shift becomes permanent, and the child loses respect for the parent.

Closer Look at Example 2: The Reward

At first glance, you might argue that Mom is still engaging in bribery. But I'm going to show you that fine detail that makes Mom retain the control in this situation.

"Molly, when you turn off the tablet, then I will reward you for following directions."

In this example, Mom engages in a *When-Then* dynamic. This is slightly different than *If-Then*. WHEN has an unspoken message of, "you *will* do this," whereas IF has the unspoken message of, "you *might* do this." IF offers room for the child to say *no*, whereas WHEN offers no room for disagreement. WHEN is a command. IF is a plea.

Now, this doesn't mean that you can't successfully use *If-Then* statements with your kids. *If-Then* statements can be useful, but when giving commands, we want to make sure we stay in a place of control. As such, these subtle shifts in our language can make a huge difference.

Another difference in Example 2 is that Mom doesn't prematurely "show her cards" to Molly. The second part of her statement simply offers a "reward," but it doesn't give away what that reward is. Here's why that can be important....

Let's say Molly isn't motivated by staying up late. In Example 1, Mom reveals this potential reward to Molly. If Molly wasn't motivated by this reward, she would continue to play on her tablet. Why would she stop for something that doesn't motivate her?

Consider your own behavior for a moment.... Let's say you were offered an additional, monetary incentive at work for working longer hours, and your company shared that the incentive is $1 for an extra hour of work. Chances are, $1 isn't going to motivate you, so you're not going to bother. You'd rather go home. Same idea applies to Molly.

Keeping the reward a mystery means Mom doesn't place herself at risk of Molly snubbing the incentive. Additionally, by revealing the reward at the onset, this opens the table up for bargaining, which is something you don't want as a parent. We will discuss bargaining further along in this chapter.

Consequences vs Punishment

Now that we've figured out how to give effective rewards, our last step is to understand consequences. Just like most parents are engaging in *bribing* instead of *rewarding*, I find many parents are administering *punishments* instead of *consequences*. Like before, the difference lies in the fine lines. To better understand the difference, we will take a closer look at the definitions of each one. By googling each term, the following definitions came up:

- **Consequence**- "a result or effect of an action or condition" ("Consequence," def. 1)

- **Punishment**- "the infliction or imposition of a penalty as retribution for an offense" ("Punishment," def.1)

Hopefully, you can already see the differences between these terms. When I teach this topic to parents in family therapy, I coach them to think of it as a "state of mind."

When we are *punishing* our kids, we are often trying to exert our power over them. There is typically a punitive quality to the disciplinary session and a subconscious desire for retribution. In most cases, if someone were to ask you why you administered that specific punishment and how that punishment links back to the offense, you probably would come up with a pretty lame answer.

When we are administering *consequences*, on the other hand, you know exactly why you are giving that specific consequence and how that consequence links back to your child's offense. The flavor of your disciplinary session is instructional in nature, and links back to our Parenting Philosophy of being your child's first and most influential teacher. Every time your child makes a mistake, it's a teachable moment. If you just administer a consequence but don't talk to your child about what happened and what you expect to see differently, then you lose the opportunity for them to grow and learn. Consequences should always come with a thoughtful discussion between you and your child (I'll give you some tips for this in the *Efficient Communication* section of this chapter). Finally, *consequences* tend to be a natural result of your child's behavior. It makes sense, is logical, and is fair.

Bargaining and Negotiations

Before we move on to the next section of this chapter, I wanted to briefly touch on the topic of bargaining and negotiating with your kids. Have you ever experienced your child negotiating with you? In our previous example, Molly could have easily stated, "*I want to stay up for 30 minutes.*" This becomes a slippery slope when we start talking about power dynamics and control in the home. Just like *If-Then* statements, allowing your child to negotiate or bargain with you about things is not necessarily bad. In fact, it can be a positive thing in your home. But, once again, there is a time and place for these types of dynamics. If you are running late to work/school, the last thing you want to do is get into a bargaining match with your kid.

Bargaining is also a dynamic better reserved for older kids, and not when you are working with toddlers or very young children. In these early years, you are trying to teach your children how to listen and follow directives while establishing the power dynamics in your home. Young children require structure and very clear directives, which is another reason why posted family rules can be so helpful. Negotiating doesn't provide that. It's a gray area, and most young children aren't cognitively ready to understand or manage this type of dynamic.

If you have a child who has proven to be responsible, mature, and well behaved, you can consider allowing bargaining because your child has EARNED it. Children who struggle with healthy boundaries, don't follow directions easily, are immature, or frequently misbehave are not good candidates for negotiating. These children require cleaner, clear lines that are more "black and white." The grey areas of bargaining will only confuse them and set you both up for frequent frustration and arguing.

Exercise: Respond

Do you remember that list of family rules you came up with? It's time to pull that list out again. For this exercise I want you to determine the consequence for each rule that is broken. There are 2 requirements:

1. Make the consequence developmentally appropriate.

2. Make sure the consequence links back to "the crime." We are looking for consequences that are natural and logical given the rule that is broken.

Let's look at an example. Let's say the rule is:

Be respectful to others at all times.

First, notice that this rule touches one of the cornerstones of our parenting philosophy (i.e. *Respect for All*). For family members older than 6-years-old, you might decide the consequence for breaking this rule is:

Write an apology letter to the person you disrespected.

For children under the age of 6, you might remove them from the situation for a period of time and bring them back to verbally apologize for their behavior. If you have a pre-verbal child, you might remove them from the situation and then bring them back to engage in a physical display of apology. For example, when my kids were babies, I would take their hand and gently pat the person we were apologizing to while saying "I'm sorry for hurting you."

Notice how this consequence encompasses several factors we have discussed in this book:

1. It's links back to the rule being broken.
2. You're replacing the behavior you *don't* want to see (i.e. disrespect) with one that you *do* want (i.e. being able to apologize and seek forgiveness).
3. It's developmentally appropriate.
    - The pre-verbal child uses gestures as a way to apologize.

- ○ The young verbal child uses words to apologize.
- ○ The older child who has mastered written language uses verbal or written words to apologize.

Now it's your turn! Go through each rule and determine what the consequence for breaking each rule will be. Remember that, whatever the consequence is, if you break the rule, you'll need to follow through with the consequence for yourself too! If you have a co-parent, make sure you collaborate with them and that they are on board too!

List your rule and then write out the consequence for that rule. You can use the space provided for this exercise or you can type it up on the computer.

_____

_____

_____

_____

_____

_____

_____

_____

_____

_____

Determining your consequences ahead of time helps to make sure you don't become reactive. Many times, we can punish too harshly if we are overwhelmed. By having our consequences pre-determined, we can be more conscientious in our parenting and make sure we aren't over-reacting in the moment. It also helps to make sure we are being fair to all children in the home and improves our consistency in enforcing rules from day-to-day, between co-parents, and from child-to-child. We'll cover all of this in the next section.

9.2 Parents

Now that we've looked at the broader environment of your home, it's time to hone down and look at what you, as a parent, need to do to provide wholistic and effective discipline to your children. In this section, we'll look at the following topics:

- Conscientious Parenting vs Reactive Parenting
- Parental Consistency
- Efficient Communication
- Parental Warmth & Affection
- Structure of Disciplinary Sessions

As a parent, you must be consistent, be a clear communicator, firm, warm, and affectionate. We will look at each of these components in greater detail, and you will see how they come together to form a competent, effective, and loving parent.

Conscientious Parenting vs Reactive Parenting

Let me start off by saying that Conscientious Parenting is what you are aiming for, but it is not easy to master. Parenting from this state of mind is hard, and the reality is, none of us can parent from this place ALL THE TIME. It's impossible! We are all human, and we are going to make some mistakes. As long as you are able to accept them and take steps to improve yourself, it will all be ok. With that said, let's take a deeper dive into the differences between Conscientious and Reactive Parenting.

Reactive Parenting is whenever you are parenting from an emotional state (namely when you are angry). When parenting from this place, you are more likely to yell, discipline harshly, and may find yourself saying things like "You are a bad boy," and so on. These are not our finest moments as parents... and we are all guilty of them. We all do this at some point in our parenting career. Just be honest with yourself, recognize it when it happens, and then correct the mistake. The more you do this, the better you will get at it, and the less you'll be parenting from that state of mind.

In contrast, **Conscientious Parenting** is when you are in control of your emotions. Your words and actions are thought out carefully, and your interactions with your child have purpose and meaning to them. During disciplinary sessions, you know exactly why you are giving a specific consequence, and you know how that consequence links back to your child's offense. This doesn't mean that you don't get angry, hurt, frustrated, and so on. Rather, you are *in control* of these emotions, and they do not govern your actions. Conscientious Parenting is a skill, and it takes consistent effort on our part to master it.

Exercise: Reflect

Do you think you are more of a reactive parent or a conscientious parent? Some of us tend to lean a little more on the reactive side, while others lean more on the conscientious side. Which one are you? Remember, be honest with yourself. No one will see the answer but you! Complete the sentence.

As a parent, I tend to be more...

Conscientious   Reactive

In truth, we've all had moments where we are reactive or where we are conscientious. None of us are perfect and none of us get it right all the time. That's why it's important to help ourselves by doing things like pre-determining the consequences for broken family rules. A little effort now helps us a whole bunch later when we are under stress and overwhelmed with the troubles of the world. Remember, in order to know where you are going, you need to know where you are starting from. Whatever you circled above, that's your starting point. The first step of any journey of self-growth is awareness.

Parental Consistency

Parental Consistency is one of those drums that practically every parenting expert beats. Most parenting books speak endlessly on the need to be consistent as a parent, and with good reason! It plays a huge part in behavior modification and, if you can't learn to be consistent as a parent, you'll find that behavioral problems will plague you for years to come!

After working with thousands of families over the course of my career, I've come to see that many parents *know* that they have to be consistent, but often don't *realize* that they aren't. Do you think you are consistent in your own parenting? Have you ever thought about it before? Take a moment to consider it now. Are you a consistent parent?

Most parents don't realize that Parental Consistency has multiple parts. There are 3 parts, in fact, and we're going to take a look at all 3. As a parent, you (and whoever your co-parent is if you have one), must master these 3 components in order to really check this one off. They are:

1. Consistency from day to day
2. Consistency between co-parents
3. Consistency between children

Consistency is critical. As we go through each one, take the time to be honest with yourself. Ask yourself: Is there any way that I can improve with these items?

Consistency Day by Day

Our first component is about being consistent each day of the week. This means that if you have a specific rule in your home that you would like followed, you must be up to the task of enforcing this rule throughout the day and throughout *each* day of the week. On the surface, this component seems extremely basic and easy to follow, but it is one of the trickiest to manage successfully.

To illustrate, let's look at an example:

It is Saturday morning, and you have a rule of "no jumping on the couch." As your child races to the living room to begin his day, he immediately hops onto the sofa with glee and begins bouncing. As you pour your cup of coffee, you give him a warning to stop bouncing on the couch or he'll have a consequence. He stops jumping, but an hour later, begins jumping on the couch again. You give another warning, but this time, he doesn't comply, and you administer a consequence. Five hours later, after spending time outside, he returns to the living room, hopping around once again on the sofa. You give him another warning and end up having to give him a consequence in the end. This time, however, he has a meltdown about the consequence, and your patience is starting to run thin. Imagine that this same routine keeps going on into the night. Now, you are emotionally and physically exhausted, and once again your child is jumping on the sofa.

Most of you know that, no matter how tired you are, you have to be consistent, you have to give out your warnings, and you have to follow through with the appropriate discipline. The truth is, few of us have the energy to keep fighting this tired battle. Furthermore, imagine that this example took place during the week after a long hard day at work. You are even less likely to be consistent and follow through. Hopefully you can see that this component, though easy to understand, is actually much more challenging to meet.

Consistency Between Co-Parents

As a parent, most of us have someone that we are parenting our children with. Your co-parent may be your spouse, your own parents, an aunt or uncle, caregiver, and so on. **Co-parents** are those individuals who are responsible for watching your children a significant amount of the time. If I were to use myself as an example, my co-parents are my husband and my own parents (who babysit daily while we finish our day at work).

For this item, we are looking at consistency among all of your co-parents, especially if you all live in the same household. This means all co-parents share the same expectations of your children and are enforcing the same rules. It doesn't have to be exactly the same, however, just similar. For children, when co-parents stay consistent between each other, our children feel a greater sense of security and stability, and they are better able to meet our expectations of them. When you are consistent from co-parent to co-parent, the likelihood is that your child will be more compliant and meet your expectations more regularly.

Finally, parents must be consistent between one another. This means they must be on the same page and be supportive of one another throughout the disciplinary process. Failure to do so will create alliances between children and specific co-parents. Think of a time when your child might have said, "Well *Dad* lets me do it," or "Grandma *always* lets me have soda with breakfast." These are examples of situations where co-parents are not parenting similarly, and so it leads to alliances between the child and that co-parent. This is an example of *triangulation*, a concept we will discuss in more detail in chapter 10. On the surface, this can seem harmless, but consider how many arguments stem from these types of scenarios. Furthermore, this leads to disruptions in the power dynamics of the home. In these situations, the child may gain more authority than one parent because the child has formed an alliance with the opposite parent. Tackling co-parenting problems is a big task, and we'll dive a little deeper in chapter 10.

Consistency Between Children

Households with multiple children need to establish consistency from one child to the next. This means that if you're disciplining your oldest child for misbehaving, you need to discipline your youngest child for engaging in that same behavior too. Consequences should be given to both children, but they should be developmentally appropriate for your child's age and maturity level. It is important for your children to see the rules applied equally among all children in the home; this demonstrates that you are remaining consistent from child to child. This will decrease the likelihood that your children will experience sibling rivalries. Many sibling rivalries arise because children feel they are being treated differently from their brother and/or sister. As such, this creates feelings of resentment towards their sibling (and sometimes their parents), which then develops into jealousy.

***

Believe it or not, collaboratively developing your list of family rules and consequences with your co-parent just took you leaps ahead on conquering parental consistency! Not only did it help you align your parenting with your co-parent, but it will help you parent more consistently between your children and from day to day! So, if you skipped those exercises in the previous section because it felt like too much work, now's your time to go back and get them done. Trust me, you don't want to skip that step!

Efficient Communication

Clear communication is an important social skill, plays a vital role in relationships, and is definitely a foundational building block for effective discipline. You must become a clear communicator. This means that your child must clearly understand what the expectations are for his behavior. Having your family rules written down and on display is one of the ways that you can improve your communication. Not only does it help you be on the same page with your co-parent, but it reduces the "I didn't know" argument that so many older kids *love* using.

It's hard to argue that you were unaware of a rule if it is clearly written down and on display. The act of having your family rules written out clearly also helps to improve consistency between co-parents and between children.

Children should also have a clear understanding of what the rewards and consequences are for their behavior. Remember, consequences and rewards should be developmentally appropriate for your child's age and intellectual abilities. When lecturing or communicating to your children, consider the following 8 tips:

1. Go down to your child's eye level- This means that you should either sit on the floor or kneel in front of your child so that you can look at each other in the eye. Do your best to avoid your child having to look up at you and you down at them.

2. Speak slowly, clearly, and calmly- It's important to explain things slowly while also using a firm tone. Try your best to remain calm and keep the volume of your voice down (or to an appropriate level). If your child is upset, screaming at your child will only increase the chances that they will scream right back at you. Modeling calm communication will help your child to calm down too.

3. Use developmentally appropriate words and concepts- Be sure that you break down larger, more complex concepts (if needed) for younger children. I have found that children work well with metaphors. Using metaphors help to create pictures in your child's mind of the lesson you are trying to teach which helps to retain these lessons. If you use a word that seems large or complex, ask your child if they know what the word means. If they say *yes*, ask them to explain the word to you to make sure their understanding of the word/concept is correct. Don't just assume your child understands. Take the opportunity to teach them and help expand their vocabulary!

4. Avoid sarcasm in your communications- Young children don't understand sarcasm well and will most likely be confused by what you are trying to express. Sarcasm will also model poor behavior for your older children and will increase the likelihood that your teen will respond to you with sarcasm in the future. Would you like it if your teen responded to you with sarcasm? Would you consider it disrespectful? Would a teacher at school consider it disrespectful? It's just best practice to avoid this as best as you can during disciplinary sessions.

5. Be specific- When praising your child, be sure to affirm a specific behavior, be specific with the behavior you want replaced, and be specific with the behavior that you want to see instead. The more specific you are and the more consistent you are in being specific, the higher the likelihood you will see an increase or decrease in the behaviors you want changed. *Specificity* is one of the most important parts of being an efficient communicator. Mastering this alone will do wonders to improve your child's behavior and the efficacy of your disciplinary sessions. To really grasp this tip, let's look at an example:

Sample 1: *"Stop doing that! I don't like it when you do that."*

This sample is way too vague, and kids are amazing at playing dumb. I guarantee that giving commands or corrections in this way will only lead to frustration for everyone involved. In contrast, try giving your directives like this:

> **Sample 2:** *"Stop yelling, please. I don't like it when you yell. Speak to me calmly and quietly so that I can understand you."*

In Sample 2, you are stating the behavior you want to see stopped (*yelling*), and you are being specific with the behavior you want to see it replaced with (*speaking calmly and quietly*). This sample leaves no room for arguing and no room to play dumb. The child knows exactly what you want to see stopped and what you want to see instead.

6. Label the behavior, *not* the child- It is common for parents to say something such as, *"Stop doing that. You are being a bad boy!"* This is an example of labeling the child because you are calling the child a *bad boy*. When doing this, you are making a statement about your child's character. We want to avoid doing that as much as possible. Hearing statements like the one above can contribute to a poor self-esteem over the course of time. A better way to tackle this might be saying something like, *"Stop yelling. Yelling is not the best choice."* In this example, you are highlighting that the behavior is the problem, not the child. You are also being specific with the behavior you want to see stopped (*yelling*).

7. Highlight *"choice"* whenever possible and appropriate- The power of *choice* can be important in parenting. From the toddler years and on, children appreciate the ability to make their own choices, which helps them to develop independence. It is clearly important to provide our children with choices, but only when appropriate. When it comes to discipline, *choice* has a role to play as well. As mentioned previously in this chapter, semantics and word-choice are powerful in parenting. Let's take another look at the examples given above:

"Stop yelling. Yelling is not the best choice."

In this example, not only are we being *specific* and avoiding an attack on our child's character, but we are also highlighting *choice*. We are implying to our child that their behavior is a choice. If the behavior is a choice, then the child has the power, capacity, and capability to make a *different* choice. This is empowering to your child, highlights the control that they have over their own behavior, and helps to instill ownership and accountability in our children.

8. When giving directives, use the 4 W's- Try to include the 4 W's into your directives: Who, What, Where, and When. Here is an example of a good, clear directive:

"Tommy, in 5 minutes, I need you to put on your shoes by the front door."

In this example, Tommy (*The Who*) has been given one directive (*The What:* put on shoes) with a clear expectation of when (*The When:* in 5 minutes) and where (*The Where:* the front door) the task should be done. This directive is clear with the 4 W's of the situation. Although Tommy may not follow through with this directive perfectly, the likelihood of the directive being followed through in the manner expected by the parent is greatly increased.

Practicing efficient and clear communication will improve how well your child responds and complies with your requests and directives. You will see an improvement in behavior from your child and a reduction in frustration and irritability because your child clearly understands what is expected from him. Furthermore, they know what they can do to improve their behavior. This increases the chance that they will meet your expectations in the future.

Parental Warmth & Affection

As a parent, you need to be firm, warm, and affectionate. In this section, we are going to look at how warmth and affection are used in disciplinary sessions. In chapter 4, we discussed the Parent-Child Relationship and its importance in happy and emotionally healthy families. In many ways, the Parent-Child Relationship is intimately intertwined with a wholistic disciplinary approach. As such, you might find that information discussed in chapter 4 and in this section will be similar. The purpose of reviewing this information is to help you better understand how the Parent-Child Relationship has a role in disciplinary sessions and vice versa. With that said, let's look at how you can use warmth and affection in our wholistic disciplinary approach.

Praise

It is a known fact that children want to please their parents, and they crave the attention of their primary caregivers. If children can't gain attention from their parents by behaving in positive ways, they will purposefully engage in negative behaviors. Children would much rather have negative attention from you than no attention at all! This boggles most parents who I work with, and perhaps seems counter-intuitive to you now.

Have you ever noticed that when your child is behaving appropriately, keeping himself entertained, you may not interact with him at all? Perhaps you wash dishes, fold laundry, or accomplish other ordinary tasks. Yet, when your child is misbehaving, you will drop everything that you are doing to address the problem. This is an example of where children will often get more attention from us for misbehaving than they do for behaving appropriately. This creates a dynamic where a child, in order to gain our attention, will purposefully engage in behavior that they know will get them in trouble because they know it will gain our attention.

So, I'll repeat this important concept once more: *children would rather have negative attention from us than no attention at all.* This dynamic begins early on in infancy when we leave babies alone in a swing or playing with toys while we try to accomplish household tasks (or just take a much-needed break!). You aren't being negligent, and this is certainly not the mark of a bad parent, but it does set us up for the dynamic described above. The question then becomes, how can we correct this situation? How can we utilize this same dynamic to encourage positive behavior? The answer is... *praise* often!

Praise is a type of reward that we give our children for a job well done. When your child brings home good grades from school, you praise them, right? If they did a great job in a soccer game, you praise them, correct? It is a reward and is often the *best* reward you can give your child.

Praising often will create a dynamic where children feel good about themselves, and they will want to continue to feel that way. They also see that they gain your favor and attention. As such, they will want to behave appropriately more often in order to gain more attention (*Sound familiar?*). Essentially, the more you focus on good behavior, the more often good behavior will happen. It's that easy!

Despite the simplicity of this concept, it is probably one of the most difficult ones to follow through with. As parents, we are often overwhelmed with the demands of everyday life. We are all guilty of racing from one task to the next without stopping to think about what our children need from us. As such, we set up the dynamic described above, where we go from task to task and pay little attention to when our children are behaving well and appropriately. It takes hard work to develop a habit of recognizing your child when they are behaving well.

The good news is, all praise is good! Whatever you can muster is going to help you. Like many other concepts in this chapter, however, there are tips that you can follow to improve and maximize the effectiveness of your praise. Take a look at the following tips:

1. Praise specific behaviors- Just like with communication, the more specific, the better! By being specific on what behavior you are praising, your child will have a better understanding of what to do again in the future. For example, saying *"I love how gently you played with the baby"* is more informative for your child than *"Good job!"* Another example might be, *"Thank you for listening to Mommy the first time I asked you."* This praise is better than, *"Thank you for listening,"* because you are highlighting that you appreciate being listened to the first time as opposed to the 10th.

2. Be sincere and enthusiastic in your praise- Non-verbal communication, such as smiling, thumbs up, and high fives are a nice added touch to your praise, especially for young children. Don't let your teen fool you, however. They might roll their eyes at your thumbs-up, but they secretly enjoy your enthusiasm for their accomplishment.

3. Avoid criticism when praising- Many of us are guilty of this. Have you ever said something like, *"Great job on your homework! Why can't you do it like this all the time?"* This is called a *back-handed compliment.* Has anyone ever complimented you in this way? It doesn't feel sincere, and the critique at the end can cancel out the praise. Here's another example, *"You look nice today. Why can't you always dress this nice?"* Ouch! Say this one to your teen daughter, and you'll probably end up with a door slammed in your face. Stick with the compliment and then bite your tongue after!

4. Praise immediately following behavior- Do your best to reward your child with your praise as soon as you catch them in the act. This helps to ensure that your child is connecting the praise with the behavior that you are trying to increase. If you can't catch them in the act, praise as soon as you are able. Just be sure to explain to your child what they are being praised for. Be as specific as you can!

Remember that *praise* is a type of reward. Use it frequently! Not only does it help increase those behaviors you want to see, but it also helps develop a positive Parent-Child Relationship. You'll be depositing funds into that Emotional Piggy Bank we discussed in chapter 4, and the best part is it's FREE! So, layer on the praise!

Structure of Disciplinary Sessions

I spent much time considering whether or not I would provide specific disciplinary techniques in this book, such as time-outs, removal of privileges, etc. In the end, I decided that diving into specific parenting strategies would retract from the primary purpose of this text: to teach you foundational parenting skills that you could apply throughout your child's lifespan. As such, I shied away from providing you with specific discipline techniques. Instead, we will focus on the structure of disciplinary sessions. You will find this last part will encompass everything we have discussed so far in this section of the chapter. It all comes together, which is why this part is last.

When you have determined a need to discipline your child, you have begun a **disciplinary session**. It includes how you approach your child, what you say to them, and what consequences you administer. In short, it is the actual process of disciplining your child from start to finish. Regardless of what disciplinary technique you use, the effectiveness of your discipline is largely determined by *how* you implement it. Keeping in mind everything we've discussed in this chapter so far, we are going to break the disciplinary session into 3 parts:

1. Presentation
2. Implementation
3. The Wrap-Up

You're going to see how, by combining everything you've learned so far, you can accomplish effective discipline without shame, all while improving your Parent-Child Relationship by establishing mutual respect between you and your child.

Presentation

How you enter a disciplinary session is really going to set the tone for how the whole session is going to turn out. If you enter the disciplinary session with anger, frustration, resentment, etc., your child is going to sense that. Remember our discussion on Conscientious Parenting vs Reactive Parenting? This is where that comes into play. You must be in control of your emotions. If you come into the disciplinary session from a reactive place, you will trigger an immediate emotional response from your child before you ever even start talking. This response may be shame, guilt, anger, or defiance.

Coming into the disciplinary session in a calm manner is going to be a critical first step. If you can manage compassion, this will greatly add a soothing effect to the disciplinary session. You also want to remain firm. Being firm is going to send the message to your child that the situation is serious, and you aren't playing games. Finally, enter the session with the mindset that this is a teachable moment. This will help keep down the sense of guilt or shame your child might begin to feel. Express to your child that you are there to teach them alternate behaviors that are going to get them better results.

Implementation

Implementation is all about how you conduct the disciplinary session. It's essentially the "lecture" portion of your chosen disciplinary method. Ideally, you are going to wait until your child has calmed down enough that they are able to listen. When your child is in the height of a temper tantrum, that's not the time to lecture. In this situation, you're going to want to wait until he has settled down and can focus on you. This is, generally, when sending your child to a quiet space or separating them from the situation that is causing them distress is a good idea. Remember, though, that when you remove them from the space, you should be doing this in a calm manner (i.e. *Presentation*).

During the implementation portion of your session, you'll want to remember all of those tips we learned when we discussed *efficient communication*. This is when your communication skills are put to the test, as well as your ability to remain *conscientious* in your word-choice and in your consequences. Know *what* you are saying and *why* you are saying it. Stay in control of yourself and do your best to not become reactive.

Once your child is calm enough, you should begin the lecture portion of the disciplinary session. Now, when I say "lecture," I don't mean that you talk at your kids. You should be trying to engage them in a dialogue where they can explain to you their side of the story, their own emotions, and express their thought processes. This is important. It shows your child that you care about their opinions and "their side" of the story (particularly important with pre-teens and teens). Be patient as you listen, reflect what you hear often, and truly try to understand the situation from their perspective.

During this dialogue, be sure that you are helping your child to identify their emotions (*"Sounds like you were pretty angry at your brother"*), and help your child to understand how their behavior has affected other people (*"When you yelled at your brother, I think he might have felt embarrassed,"*). Doing this helps to develop empathy, compassion for others, and grows your child's emotional maturity. Remember to present these emotions in a calm way to help encourage the dialogue and keep down any potential feelings of shame or resentment or picking sides.

Finally, be specific when discussing the behavior you disapprove of, and be specific in what you would like to see next time. Encourage your child to think of alternative behaviors that they can try with you. This is a great practice because you are modeling problem-solving skills to them, as well as critical thinking. For younger kids, you'll need to provide these alternative behaviors to them.

The Wrap-Up

It is important for us to remember that kids are always going to make mistakes. They are new to this world, and their ability to assess the consequences of their behaviors is not fully developed. After all, even as adults, we *still* make mistakes. Don't we all deserve a little grace then?

When ending our disciplinary sessions, we should remain calm and firm, but also display empathy, warmth, and affection. Being able to display these emotions and behaviors goes back to modeling, whereby showing yourself as being calm, firm, and empathetic helps your child to learn and reflect the same behaviors back to you during times of stress. Being calm, firm, and empathetic also models graciousness, and will allow your children to actually *listen* to you because they aren't zeroing in on the volume or tone of your voice.

Finally, when ending the disciplinary session, always end with an *Act of Love*. All kids want to know that, even though they have displeased you or have hurt someone in their family, they are still loved. It is very important to make sure that your child feels loved and accepted by you, regardless of their behavior. One way to accomplish this is by ending the disciplinary session with an Act of Love, such as a hug or a kiss from you. Let your child know that, no matter what, you will always love them! I cannot emphasize the importance of this enough. This helps to reaffirm for your child that they are still loved, wanted, and accepted by you regardless of the mistakes that they may have made. This is the *Parental Warmth & Affection* component at its best, and it helps to repair any minor damage caused to the Parent-Child relationship by the disciplinary session. When disciplining siblings, you can encourage them to give each other a hug, shake hands, or anything else that would help to display love towards one another. This powerful act helps to reaffirm to your child that they are inherently "good" (something we discussed in our Parenting Philosophy section) and worthy of love. This helps to further emphasize that the behavior is the problem, not the child.

9.3 Final Thoughts on Discipline

I hope that this detailed and thorough look at discipline has been helpful. We started off broad by looking at your overall home environment and then honed it down to you. We discussed tips for more effective discipline, tips for better communication, and broke down the disciplinary session into 3 parts. Hopefully, you can see how everything has come together and has formed a cohesive picture.

Now, I know some individuals will be disappointed that I didn't address specific parenting techniques in this chapter or discuss other related topics such as managing power struggles. The reality is, there are hundreds of books that do a wonderful job of tackling these topics. If you feel, however, that you want my specific spin on these concepts, you can check out my website at: kcdreisbach.com. My blog covers all of it! Not only will you find some of the items discussed in this book, but you'll find help on more nuanced items such as:

- How to manage power struggles
- How to manage anger outbursts and temper tantrums
- How to get your kids to listen the first time you ask
- How to manage sibling rivalries

That's just a taste of what you can find there. There is so much more! So, forgive me for not diving deep into specific parenting techniques, but please help yourself to the abundance of parenting articles on my website.

10

Co-Parenting

Pretty much every family has a co-parent. For a single mom, the co-parent might be her chosen caregivers or a daycare worker. For a couple who is raising their children together, they both are co-parents. For me, my co-parents are my husband and my own parents. Every family is different. A co-parent is essentially anyone who is parenting your child for a large portion of the time.

These people, due to how much time they spend raising your child, are also responsible for the outcome! They are contributing to who your child becomes in adulthood. Your co-parents are invested in your child whether the investment is emotional (such as a grandparent), biological (such as the birth mother or father), marital (as in stepparents), fiscal (as in daycare workers). It doesn't matter how; these people are invested, and because they spend so much time with your child, they are contributing to the emotional, moral, and behavioral development of the child.

In an ideal co-parenting situation, the co-parents share common/ similar views on everything. They share the same household rules, the same discipline style, the same rewards, the same values, same morals and ethics, and the same life lessons, etc. Essentially, that co-parent is an extension of you! This, however, is rarely the reality. The reality is far messier and a lot trickier to manage.

In most co-parenting situations, no one agrees on everything. It is a messy process, frustrating, and totally normal. Most parents find themselves constantly arguing and bickering between themselves and their co-parents. The truth is that co-parenting is either going to bring you together or it is going to create dissension between you and your co-parents. If you experience dissension, then your co-parenting relationship becomes vulnerable to:

- **Triangulation** – A process by which one person in a relationship draws a third person in to help dissipate or mitigate the tension that existed in the original duo.
- **Parental Sabotage** – The act of someone undermining your parenting.

We reviewed both of these concepts in great detail in *AoP*, but I wanted to give you a quick reference here. These 2 problems can create lots of conflict in your co-parenting relationships, so it is incredibly important to work with your co-parents on preventing these disasters!

Exercise: Connect

Before we jump into potential solutions, let's first examine your co-parenting situation. Who are the co-parents in your life right now? Who are the individuals that spend a significant amount of time caring for your children? Consider some of these examples:

- Spouse/Boyfriend/Girlfriend
- Aunt/Uncle
- Grandparents
- Teacher/Coach/Daycare Worker
- Siblings
- Neighbors/Friends

Who are your co-parents at this point in time? Why?

_____

_____

_____

_____

What is the relationship that you have with each co-parent like? Do you share similar views on parenting? Are they supportive of your parenting choices? Do you ever feel as though your parenting is undermined by them? Do you think that you or your co-parent are guilty of engaging in triangulation or parental sabotage?

_____

_____

_____

_____

_____

Do you think that your co-parenting relationships need some work? Why?

Yes   No

_____

_____

_____

_____

At this point, you should have identified who your co-parents are and acknowledged if your relationship with them needs some work. If at this time, you don't have co-parents or you feel as though your relationship with them doesn't need assistance, then feel free to skip the rest of this chapter and move on. You can always come back to it in the future.

10.1 Preventing Co-Parenting Disasters

The best way to manage co-parenting disasters is to prevent them. Once you have identified who your co-parents are, you will need to determine the best way to engage and collaborate with them. Collaboration is the key and heart of healthy and effective co-parenting relationships. We'll start by examining some ways you can begin working with your primary co-parents, such as grandparents and spouses, and then we'll take a look at special groups such as teachers.

Collaborating with Primary Co-Parents

Your primary co-parent is anyone who lives in your home and takes an active part in raising the kids. This might be your spouse, grandparent, or even and adult sibling. This person is present all the time, and you rely on this person constantly to help you raise your child. This is your primary co-parent, and your goal should be aligning yourself with them as much as you can. If you are both on the same page, life just got a whole lot easier for you AND your child. But how do you get on the same page?

Back in chapter 2, you began developing your own parenting philosophy, and this has been the backbone of your work throughout this text. In that chapter, I insinuated a discussion with your co-parent on parenting philosophies, but it wasn't a specific exercise. If you had that discussion, then you're ahead of the pack. If you didn't, there's no time like the present! Just like having a parenting philosophy was important to provide structure to who you are as a parent, it is equally important when you co-parent with someone else. That's what we are going to do next, create a shared vision for your household parenting philosophy.

Exercise: Respond, Part 1

Find a time where you and your co-parent can have some uninterrupted time. You're going to engage your co-parent in a discussion about parenting philosophies. You can use chapter 2 from this book as a way to help guide and structure your conversation. Go through the following steps as a team:

1. Review my 7 Principles and see what you both agree on. Write those down on your paper.
2. Review with your co-parent your own parenting philosophy you developed in the chapter 2 *Respond* exercise. See what they agree with and add it to your list.
3. Now, ask your co-parent if there is anything they feel should be added to the list and why. What principles are important to them? Consider each principle they present and determine whether you agree on it. If you agree on it, add it to your list. If you don't, try to have a collaborative discussion about it.
4. Review your list. Hopefully, you have at least 5 principles that can guide you and your co-parent on your shared parenting journey. Remember, there is no "right or wrong" number of principles. Write down your finalized parenting philosophy below:

Our Family's Parenting Philosophy

_____

_____

_____

_____

_____

_____

_____

_____

_____

_____

Nice work! You've collaborated with your co-parent on a shared parenting vision. Remember, you both should be referring back to your family's parenting philosophy to help you make difficult decisions for your family. You should be looking to make sure that your decisions and parental actions align with this shared parenting vision.

Parenting is more than just a philosophy, it's about action. Parenting is (and should be) one of the most interactive things you do in life. As my husband used to say, "The right answer to any parenting question is usually the one that requires the most effort." This shared parenting philosophy is going to be the foundation for everything else we do in this chapter. So, if you skipped *Respond, Part 1*, then go back and complete it now. There are no shortcuts! (Sorry!) Now, we're going to begin developing the structure for your home that should help in aligning you and your co-parent.

Exercise: Respond, Part 2

For this exercise, you and your co-parent are going to formulate your household's family rules. This means you'll need to discuss what rules you expect everyone in your home (including the both of you) to follow. Remember, these rules should align with your parenting philosophy. Consider rules around chores, honesty, behavior, obedience, bedtimes, etc. Some families have 3 rules and some families have 100. It doesn't matter how many or how little you have, just make sure that you and your co-parent both agree on the rules, and that you are both able and willing to follow those rules too.

Here is a sample set of 5 family rules:

1. Everyone in the home is subject to follow all Family Rules, city, county, state, and national ordinances and laws.
2. Always be honest in your words and actions.
3. Always practice respect towards all things, including towards animals, property, and others.
4. Complete all chores by 7:00 p.m. each day.
5. Clean up after yourselves before going to bed each day.

Now it's your turn. What are your family's rules? I've given you space for 15-18 rules, but there is no minimum or maximum number of rules your family should have. Do whatever is right for your family.

Our Family's Household Rules

_____

_____

_____

_____

_____

_____

_____

_____

_____

_____

_____

_____

_____

_____

_____

Exercise: Connect

Now that you've listed out your family's rules, take a moment to consider how each rule is supporting or is aligned with your parenting philosophy. Remember, your parenting philosophy is the foundation of it all, so your philosophy should be supporting your household rules just like the foundation of a house supports the structure of the home. Everything needs to flow together. Let's look at the sample set of family rules from the previous exercise:

1. Everyone in the home is subject to follow all Family Rules, city, county, state, and national ordinances and laws. (Principle #5)
2. Always be honest in your words and actions. (Principle #7)
3. Always practice respect towards all things, including towards animals, property, and others. (Principle #7)
4. Complete all chores by 7:00 p.m. each day. (Principle #6)
5. Clean up after yourselves before going to bed each day. (Principle #6)

Notice how each rule is supported by one of the 7 principles in my parenting philosophy. Not every principle needs a rule, but every rule should be supported by one of your principles. Take the time now to review your family rules again. This time, I want you to identify which one of the principles from YOUR parenting philosophy supports your family's rules.

If you find a rule that isn't supported by a parenting philosophy, determine why this is. Does the rule contradict the principle? If it does, what needs to change: your rule or the principle? Maybe it doesn't contradict, but you just don't have a principle that supports it. Do you need to add a principle to your parenting philosophy? Go through your family rules with your co-parent, and as a team, go through these questions and make the adjustments you need to your family rules and/or shared parenting philosophy. This might take a little time, so don't rush it! The important part here is that you do this together.

***

At this point, you've created a solid foundation with your co-parent for your family, but you are far from done! Co-parenting is a complex topic with a complex solution. Just like parenting is a 24/7 type of job, so is collaborating with your co-parent. The goal of this chapter was to help you begin a positive and collaborative co-parenting relationship, but the topic is far greater than I could cover in just one chapter of a book. To finish us off with this chapter, I will provide you with one final *Respond* exercise. The goal of this exercise is to give the roadmap on how to pursue the development and growth of this collaborative co-parenting relationship.

Exercise: Respond, Part 3

Through these exercises, you've been able to develop a foundation that laid the groundwork for your future work together. Now I'm going to give you some framework on what that future growth should look like. Over the course of the next month, consider scheduling some private moments with your co-parent to have some open-minded discussions around parenting. Once you are together, discuss the following questions:

- What should consequences look like in our home?
  - Example: We will use Timeouts.

- What should rewards look like in our home?
  - Example: We will use Praise and give extra Screen Time.

- What kinds of consequences are considered "acceptable" and which ones aren't?

- ○ Example: Spanking won't be tolerated but Timeouts are fine.

- How will we handle disagreements between us?
  - ○ Example: We won't argue in front of the kids. Instead, we will let the kids know we need to discuss it privately and get back to them.

- What should we do if we can't agree on something?
  - ○ Example: If we can't agree, we'll take turns trying each other's method.

- Can we agree that if one of us is getting too angry, the other parent needs to step in? How will we accomplish this without undermining each other?
  - ○ Example: If you get too upset while disciplining, I'll put my hand on your shoulder and offer nicely to step in.

Take notes of your discussion and what you agreed on, and then try out your plan for 2 weeks. Revisit these topics and decide as a team if something needs to be changed or altered. Remember, you are collaborating and looking for what works best for YOUR family. So, keep working together to find those ideal solutions. Always remember to treat each other with respect in front of the kids and to also treat your children with respect.

If you find that you are having a lot of difficulty with your co-parent, then you should consider seeking an objective opinion. Consider hiring a family therapist, who can listen to you and your partner discuss the matter and potentially shed some clarity on the situation. Consider compromises if you have disagreements with how to approach a parenting problem.

Collaborating with Secondary Co-Parents

Most of us have secondary co-parents. These are people who are in charge of your child's care for a portion of the day, but they don't necessarily bare the weight of "raising" them. Consider individuals like grandparents that babysit for a few hours each day after school, teachers, coaches, daycare workers, etc. Collaborating with these individuals can also be important, but not in the same way.

Since your kids don't spend as much time with these individuals, they're not as responsible for your child's behavior as you and your primary co-parent are, but they can still play an important part. When you are trying to manage disruptive behaviors, it's helpful to have your secondary co-parents on board with your plan as much as possible. This helps to reinforce what you are doing at home and produces positive results more quickly.

In most situations, secondary caregivers are willing to collaborate, but there might be limitations to what they can or can't do. For example, a teacher has several other children they are responsible for at any given time. So, you may want your child to be disciplined in a certain way, but that may not be a possibility for the teacher. This is where the art of collaboration comes in. Although I won't be giving any specific exercises to practice for this section, I will give you some ideas on topics you may want to discuss with your secondary caregivers.

Share with your secondary caregiver who your child is through your eyes. It's helpful to be honest with them and yourself. For example, when the school year begins, I always try to check in with the new teacher and share with them what I already know about my daughter. Some things I share with the teacher are:

- She's a perfectionist, so she's extremely hard on herself.
- She struggles to ask for help because she gets embarrassed.
- She's even-tempered and always in a great mood.
- If she seems "snappy," it usually means something is weighing on her emotionally.

- School bores her because she usually finds the material too easy. Challenging her is key.
- She responds well to encouragement and compliments on work well done.

Sharing this kind of information can be helpful to these secondary caregivers as they learn to work with you and your child. Remember that, in the case of teachers and daycare works, etc., they work with many children every year. They might need reminders throughout the year. As a parent, don't feel afraid or embarrassed to schedule appointments to meet with your child's teacher to see how they are doing. If a problem arises, these are excellent opportunities to discuss these matters. Examples might be:

- I've noticed he is coming home from school every day looking disheveled and sad. I think someone is bullying him. Have you noticed anything? What steps should I take with the school to make sure he is safe?
- She complains every time we need to do reading. She believes she can't do it and I'm worried it's impacting her self-esteem. What can I do at home to help with this?
- Yesterday, he came home upset because his project wasn't laminated. He said that "only the good projects got laminated." I'm trying to understand what happened. Can you help me?
- I've been having some difficulty with her at home. She's been getting really upset and getting aggressive. At home, we are instituting some consequences for this behavior. Would you be able to let me know each day how she is doing at school?

Notice that all of these examples end in questions that elicit collaboration and partnership. There are no accusations, just information and questions that show the secondary caregiver you want to work as a team.

When You Hate Your Co-Parent

Sometimes, we really don't like our co-parents. This person may be your ex, an in-law, or a teacher you just can't stand. Regardless of how you feel about the secondary caregiver, your options always boil down to two:

1. Work with them
2. Find someone new

But finding someone new isn't always a realistic option. So, learning to work with those difficult co-parents is important. Do your best to approach the situation with a spirit of partnership and collaboration. You can't control them and the attitude they bring to the table, but you *can* control yourself. Remember, just like at work, you sometimes have colleagues you just can't stand, but you have to learn to work together, right? This is no different. You and your co-parents are in the business of making your child successful. You don't have to like them, but you *do* have to work with them collaboratively.

11

Parenting & Marriage

I think everyone can agree that so much affects your parenting but parenting also really affects your marriage! Your relationship with your significant other completely changes the minute you bring home a baby and you begin the journey of raising a child together. Now, when I say "marriage" I want you to understand that I'm talking about couples in a serious relationship who are raising a child together. I don't necessarily mean "marriage" in the classical sense of the word. For this chapter, when you read the word "marriage," just know that I'm talking about two people in a committed relationship.

There are several ways that parenting affects your marriage. In *AoP*, we reviewed the following culprits:

- Dissension between the couple due to differing parenting styles and/or ideas
- Shifting focus from the couple to the children
- A decrease in intimacy (whether sexual or just physical affection)
- An increase in irritability from one or both people in the relationship

In this book, we won't dive as deeply into each one of these categories as we did in *AoP*. Instead, we will focus more on where your relationship is at in these different categories, and then discuss how you can tackle rebuilding your relationship with kids.

11.1 Dissention in the Relationship

Dissension is a pretty fancy word to describe arguing. As already mentioned, adding kids into a romantic relationship can increase disagreements between the people in that relationship. These disagreements can arise over anything, including parenting styles, disciplinary techniques, how to manage caregivers, where to put the child in school, etc. Overtime, arguments take over the relationship. The more you argue, the more the story of the relationship changes, which we will discuss a little bit later. What we will discuss right now is what arguments can do to that relationship itself and the people in the relationship. Dissension and frequent arguing can leave behind bitterness, especially if you feel like you're doing all the work in the relationship. Common "Hot Topics" for couples include:

- Money/Finances
- Children/Parenting
- Family Conflict/In-Laws
- Gender Roles/Expectations

Exercise: Reflect

Take a moment to think on your relationship. In your opinion, do you think you argue frequently with one another? When you do argue, what are the topics that are constantly coming up? What are your Hot Topics?

_____

_____

_____

_____

_____

_____

When you think about your relationship with your romantic partner, do you find yourself feeling as though you do all the work? Have you ever felt like you come home, make dinner, take care of the kids, prepare lunches for the following day, do dishes, and so on, only to look over and find your partner sitting on the sofa enjoying a drink and watching their favorite TV show?

Yes   No

If you've never felt this way, do you think your spouse does? Do you suspect they feel like they are stuck doing all (or most) of the work?

Yes   No

You'll notice that for both of these questions, there is a straight "Yes or No" answer. There are no "Maybe's." The truth is, if you find yourself thinking *maybe* then the answer is really a *yes*.

Many people find themselves in this position, feeling as though they do most of the work in the home or feeling as though they argue all the time with their spouse. It's ok to feel this way from time to time, but it can become problematic if we find ourselves feeling this way chronically. This is the path to bitterness that brews within the individual and ultimately poisons the marriage.

11.2 Shifting Focus to the Kids

When we have kids, so much of our life becomes them, and we forget to nurture the relationship we have with our partner. Essentially, we become strangers to our partners over time, and we don't even notice it!

Exercise: Reflect

When was the last time you sat down with your partner and talked about them? Not the kids, not the house, not about money or in-laws, just about who they are and who they've become? No need to write your answer to this one but do try to be honest with yourself as you think on this question.

For most people, it's been a long time. Most individuals can't even remember the last time they did this! Even couples who manage to go on regular date nights find themselves talking about the kids, the house, money, etc., instead of each other.

11.3 Decreasing Intimacy

Kids also make it difficult for couples to engage in intimate moments. With a new baby, a snoopy toddler, or an anxious teenager, sex practically disappears. Body changes from pregnancy, weight gain from poor nutrition and lack of exercise, and a more hectic life can cause reduced confidence, especially for women. Stress and exhaustion tend to decrease libido creating an end result of little or no sex in the relationship.

Exercise: Reflect

How has your sex life changed with your partner since your children were born? Circle the one that best represents you.

Decrease   Increase   Same   No sex at all

Why do you think your sex life is this way at this time? Try to be specific with your answer. Consider things like:

- Time
- Space
- Children
- Libido/Desire
- Self-esteem/Self-confidence
- Satisfaction in the Relationship

_____

_____

_____

_____

_____

_____

If your sex life has improved, then good for you! Most couples indicate that their sex life worsens after kids for a variety of reasons. It's important for you to try and determine why your sex life has worsened or improved. In doing so, you'll have a better idea of what you need to work on OR what you need to try and maintain.

11.4 Change in the Marital Narrative

The last one to discuss is the change in the marital narrative. This one is closely tied to our first point discussed (i.e. dissension between both persons in the relationship). As stress increases, intimacy decreases, and more arguments arise between the couple. Both individuals become more irritable with one another, which slowly changes the narrative. Another way to think of the narrative is the story of the couple.

We've talked about narratives before, specifically the Family Narrative. Now we're going to review the Marital Narrative, and in reviewing this, we're going to complete a similar exercise that we did earlier in this book to try and gage where your Martial Narrative is currently at.

Exercise: Reflect

Take a moment to read through each word below. Circle the words that best describe your marriage overall. Try to be as honest as you can with yourself. Remember, no one is going to see this but you!

Sad   Joyful   Jealousy   Abusive   Happy   Scary   Hurt

Draining   Sickening   Ugly   Beautiful   Trusting   Loss

Angry   Sensual   Fun   Adventurous   Boring   Loving

Lost   Lonely   Companionship   Generous   Energizing

Stingy   Sexual   Intimate   Painful   Close   Affectionate

Negative   Neutral   Separate   Together   Understanding

Compassionate   Bitter   Misunderstood   Unloved   Loved

Positive   Romantic   Used   Repetitive   Gross   Distant

Look at the words you've circled. What do you notice? Are there more positive or negative words? How do the words you circled make you feel?

_____

_____

_____

_____

_____

_____

What was it like to do this exercise? Maybe it was uncomfortable to examine your romantic relationship in this way. Frequently, couples struggle with admitting that there is a problem in their marriage until the problem has become so great, there is no way they could deny it. But this is a huge issue! By the time the problem grows that big, there is little that can be done to fix it.

If you circled mostly positive words, then that's wonderful! Keep it up! But if you found that your relationship is starting to tilt more into the negative, then it's time to roll up those sleeves and get to work. Don't deny the problem, face it head-on!

11.5 Rebuilding the Marriage... with Kids!

In this section, I'm going to give you some practical exercises you can try to begin rebuilding and/or strengthen your relationship with your partner. It's important that you understand, however, that this section isn't a replacement for Couples Therapy. Doing these exercises might help rebuild your marriage, but it won't save it if your relationship is already a sinking ship. You need to seek help from a therapist if your relationship is taking on water! People hate to admit that their relationship is struggling, and so they avoid Couples Counseling until the very last minute. Couples Counseling can be very effective, but only if you don't wait until the very end to get help! The earlier you seek out a therapist and begin treatment, the better for you and your partner.

Understanding the different ways that kids can cause havoc on your marriage is important. It is also important to know, however, that having kids does not mean that your marriage is doomed. It is possible to have children with whom you have a dedicated relationship with, and also have a loving, positive relationship with your spouse. In this section, I'm going to give you a few different ways that you can begin working on your marital relationship today by improving and nourishing the relationship.

The key to rebuilding your marriage is to rebuild the marital narrative. If you recall, in previous chapters we discussed ways to improve the Parent-Child relationship. One of those ways was by improving the family narrative. Your marital relationship is no different. It should come as no surprise that the key to improving your marriage is by having a rich and positive marital narrative. Furthermore, there are several ways that you can go about improving your marital narrative. Remember that you have an Emotional Piggy Bank with your spouse. The more you argue with your spouse, for whatever the reason, the more you withdraw funds from that emotional bank account. The less time you spend with your spouse in building the relationship, such as sharing intimate moments, the less you deposit into the account. This is why the relationship begins to fade. So, once again, the key is to begin depositing more funds into the account than you withdraw. But how do you go about doing that when you're already so busy?

In *AoP*, I gave you some tips to start rebuilding your marital narrative. They included:

- **Going on a date** – Have regularly scheduled date nights, even if you only get to spend 2 hours alone together before the kids come back. Just be sure you spend this time focusing on your partner and try to avoid those Hot Topics in your conversations. Your Date Night isn't the place to introduce conflict. This is relationship-building time!

- **Being intimate** – There are more ways of being intimate with one another than having sex. Hugs, handholding, sneaking kisses, and cuddling on the sofa are all ways of displaying physical affection and being intimate. Physical touch is great for the brain and human spirit! We all like to be held when we need comfort or patted on the back when we succeed! Find ways to incorporate physical touch in your relationship daily and try your best to engage in those more intimate gestures such as kissing and snuggling. If you can find time for more sensual touches together, then totally go for it!

- **Continuously getting to know each other** – All people change with time, and your spouse is no different. We take for granted that we've had this person in our lives for such a long time that we come to believe that we know everything about them. The reality is, we don't! Just like you've changed, so have they. Make the effort to continuously get to know them over time.

- **Finding shared experiences** – As a dating couple, we have many shared experiences with our partner. As a couple with kids, those shared experiences begin to include a bunch more people! It's important to have experiences that are just for you and your spouse. Whether that's watching a TV show together, reading books together, hiking, swimming, going to the gym, etc. Find something that just the two of you can do together and try to do it on a regular basis.

- **Focusing on the positive** - Just like we should focus as much as possible on what our kids do right, we need to do the same with our spouse. This doesn't mean that we turn a blind eye to the errors the other person makes, but rather, we should choose our battles wisely, and keep it to things that are most important. After that, we should see the good our partner is capable of. Just like children react better to positive parenting techniques, so do our spouses.

- **Practicing graciousness and gratitude** - Gratitude and graciousness are an important aspect when we look at building up relationships. Gratitude allows the other person to know that you truly appreciate what they have done for you. This might be a small gesture, like washing the dishes without you having to ask, or buying you a small gift. When expressing your gratitude, suppress the urge to tell them that you are somehow undeserving of what they have done for you. You need to remember that, just like you enjoy making others happy, your spouse likes doing the same thing for you! By letting the other person know how much you appreciate and enjoy what they have done for you, you are more likely to increase this type of behavior from them. More importantly, this continues to build and enrich the marital narrative.

Barring situations of domestic violence and abuse, and assuming a regular, normal marital relationship, following these tips will truly help to build up and improve the marital relationship you have now. The best thing is you can begin doing this right now! Today, you can begin creating situations that help foster and enrich your love life with your spouse, all while raising children.

Exercise: Respond

I've given you 6 ways you can begin rebuilding your marriage. Now I want you to put what you've learned into action! For this exercise, I want you to pick 2 (if you can manage 3, that's even better) that you want to try for the next 2 weeks. It doesn't matter which ones you choose so long as you apply them as consistently as you can. Which ones are you going to try?

_____

_____

_____

_____

_____

_____

You have your chosen strategies; how are you going to begin applying them? What's your game plan? Consider things like:

- How will you help yourself remember to engage in these things?
- What will you do if you forget?
- How will you squeeze this into your daily, weekly, or monthly schedule?
- If your plan needs a babysitter, who are you going to call and ask to watch the kids?
- How are you going to hold yourself accountable to this plan?

Take the time to jot down your plan and any answers you might have to these questions.

_____

_____

_____

_____

_____

_____

_____

_____

_____

Now that you have your plan, it's time to get started. Flag this page and try out your strategies for 2 weeks and see how it goes. Once the 2 weeks are up, come back to this page and answer the following questions:

- What was the experience like for you?
- Are there any changes you have noticed in your partner or yourself since you began implementing your plan?
- Based off of the last 2 weeks, how do you feel about your relationship with your spouse? Has it improved, remained the same, or gotten worse?
- Do you want to keep doing your plan or do you want to try something different?
- Do you want to add or change anything to your plan? If yes, what will your new plan look like?

_____

_____

_____

_____

_____

_____

_____

_____

_____

Exercise: Reflect

Now that you have tried out your plan for 2 weeks, it's time to re-evaluate the words you would use to describe your romantic relationship. Take a moment to read through each word below. Circle the words that best describe your marriage overall. You may focus primarily on the last 2 weeks, but you're welcome to incorporate your relationship as a whole as well. Try to be as honest as you can with yourself. Remember, no one is going to see this but you!

Sad   Joyful   Jealousy   Abusive   Happy   Scary   Hurt

Draining   Sickening   Ugly   Beautiful   Trusting   Loss

Angry   Sensual   Fun   Adventurous   Boring   Loving

Lost   Lonely   Companionship   Generous   Energizing

Stingy   Sexual   Intimate   Painful   Close   Affectionate

Negative   Neutral   Separate   Together   Understanding

Compassionate   Bitter   Misunderstood   Unloved   Loved

Positive   Romantic   Used   Repetitive   Gross   Distant

Look at the words you've circled. What do you notice? Are there more positive or negative words? Have the words changed at all since the last time you completed this exercise? If yes, how has it changed.

_____

_____

_____

_____

_____

_____

Hopefully, doing these exercises have helped shift your relationship into a positive direction. Remember, they are not a replacement for Couples Counseling! If your relationship is really struggling, please seek help. If you found these exercises positively impacted your relationship, consider trying them again and as often as you would like. Keep depositing funds into that Emotional Piggy Bank!

For more help on improving your marriage, check out the following books:

- *The Seven Principles for Making Marriage Work* by John Gottman and Nan Silver
- *The Relationship Cure* by John Gottman and Joan DeClaire
- *10 Lessons to Transform Your Marriage* by John Gottman, Julie Schwartz, and Joan DeClaire

In our next chapter, we will be moving on to parental burnout and talking about all the different aspects that contribute to parents feeling too overwhelmed and too stressed with their home life. I'll also be tackling how to treat and prevent parental burnout in the future.

12

Managing Parental Burnout

At this point, we have traveled full circle. We've covered the following topics on our journey thus far:

- Psychosocial development in children
- Understanding how children's emotions play into their behaviors
- How to discipline our children no matter how old they are
- How to repair damaged relationships

We are now moving on to discussing parental burnout. I can't think of a parent that hasn't experienced the effects of burnout. You're exhausted emotionally and physically and feel as though you have given everything you could possibly give. You find yourself feeling hopeless, helpless, or feeling like the work never ends. That perfect parenting perception that you thought was going to be your life when you had a baby is dead and gone. Parental burnout is real, and it happens to everyone!

12.1 What is Parental Burnout?

Parental burnout can happen for a variety of reasons, but seldom is just one problem the cause. Usually, parents become burnt out because of all those spinning plates we talked about in Chapter 1. It's the volume and chronicity of it all that overwhelms parents and creates the burnout effect. In *AoP*, we took a look at some of the things that lead parents down Burnout Road. They were:

- **Poor Eating Habits** – Drinking too much caffeine, not enough water, too much junk food, or skipping meals all together!
- **Poor Sleep** – Going to bed too late, being disturbed frequently throughout the night, and getting up too early, resulting in poor sleep quality and just too little of it all together!
- **Familial Stress** – It's all the stressors of parenthood combined! It's managing your housework, dealing with family drama, navigating your child's school and schoolwork, and dealing with your child's mood swings and behaviors. It just gets to be too much!
- **Work Stress** – We didn't even touch on this one in *AoP*! But if you work a job (whether in or out of the home), it's just another Energy Sucker pulling on your reserves. You're managing deadlines, workplace drama, and an ever-increasing To-Do List with expectations that you worry you just might not meet. Yikes!

Exercise: Reflect

Consider yourself for a moment and answer the following questions[1] as honestly as you can. When answering these questions, consider how you have been feeling over the past 2 weeks.

1. Do you find yourself having more difficulties in your significant relationships?

Yes   No

2. Do you feel more irritable or feel as though you have less patience
throughout the day?

Yes   No

3. When engaging in enjoyable activities, do you feel like the activity
provides less joy than it used too?

Yes   No

4. Are you drinking more alcohol, smoking more, or using prescription medications more frequently to help manage your stress?

Yes   No

5. Do you eat more than you used to or less than you used to?

Yes   No

6. Are you struggling to fall asleep at night? Or do you find yourself
consistently waking in the middle of the night?

Yes   No

7. Do you feel lonely or feel as though you have no one you can count
on?

Yes   No

8. Do you find yourself feeling frequently anxious?

Yes   No

9. Do you feel like your thoughts are racing or that you can't get negative thoughts out of your head?

Yes   No

If you found yourself saying yes to 4 or more of these questions, you might be experiencing parental burnout. This is a great questionnaire you can take whenever you are concerned you might be getting overwhelmed with parenting and life in general. If you find yourself responding "yes" to 8 or 9 of these questions, you might be suffering from a mental health condition, such as depression. In that case, consider meeting with a licensed mental health professional to discuss your symptoms and develop a plan to help address these concerns.

Exercise: Connect

Now that we've assessed ourselves to see where we are at with parental burnout, let's look a little closer at our experiences. If you are not experiencing burnout at this time, I encourage you to try and complete this exercise by envisioning your future self. Which categories do you feel are contributing to your parental burnout? Circle all that apply.

Poor Eating Habits

Poor Sleep

Familial Stress

Work Stress

For those categories that you circled, which one is the greatest contributor to your burnout? Why?

_____

_____

_____

_____

_____

12.2 Treating & Preventing Parental Burnout

As the famous sports quote goes, "The key to a good offense is a good defense." The good news for us as parents is that the way to help treat parental burnout is also the same way you help prevent it. This means that if you are already burned out, there are steps that you can take that will help you to feel refreshed and motivated again on your parenting journey. Furthermore, these same steps will help to prevent future burnout. In *AoP*, we dived into several ways to help manage and prevent burnout. Here's a brief reminder of what we covered:

1. Caring for Your Body [2] – Your physical body needs to be maintained. Without it, you'll end up getting sick! None of us are any good when we're ill. Be sure to:

    1. Get plenty of rest

2. Eat *something*, but try to make it healthy

3. Maintain basic hygiene like showering and brushing those teeth

4. Get some exercise, even if it's only doing some stretches in the morning

2. Caring for Your Mind[3] – Your mind powers everything, right? It's the gas in your car that keeps your motor running. Failure to take care of your mind is like trying to drive a car when the fuel tank is on empty. You're not going to go anywhere. To help care for your mind and fill that tank up with some gas, be sure to:

1. Engage in some relaxation

2. Take Mental Health Days

3. Vent out your frustrations with a friend

4. Show yourself some love

5. Speak kindly to yourself

6. Engage in Gratitude Exercises

7. Practice your faith (if you have one)

By re-envisioning self-care in this way, we are better able to conceptualize how we can incorporate it affordably and realistically into our busy lives. The key to great self-care is folding regular acts of self-love into your daily life, whether through gestures or positive words. The more you do this, the more it becomes a habit, and the easier it will be. The easier it becomes, the more frequently you will do it, creating a habitual cycle that works in your favor and improves your self-esteem, mental health, and overall well-being. Another benefit is that you are modeling self-love and self-care to your child! This will help them to develop these healthy habits too, which is going to improve their emotion regulation and self-esteem. It's a win-win for everyone!

Exercise: Respond

Look back at your response to the *Connect* exercise. I want you to pick one thing you can begin doing tomorrow to help treat or prevent parental burnout. Whatever it is you choose, try to make sure that it directly combats the category you feel is most greatly affecting you. Let's look at some examples.

Sample 1

- **Category**- Work Stress
- **Treatment Strategy**- I'm going to make sure I take my breaks at work. While on my break, I'm going to practice a relaxation technique.

Sample 2

- **Category**- Poor Eating Habits
- **Treatment Strategy**- I'm going to stop skipping breakfast. Instead, I'm going to drink a protein shake or a smoothie for breakfast.

Now it's your turn! What is going to be your strategy for combating your greatest stressor?[4] You can pick as many treatment strategies as you want, but don't overwhelm yourself! For the purposes of this exercise, I want you to pick at least one that you can try consistently for 2 weeks. Jot down your plan, along with the 1st day you are going to apply this strategy.

_____

_____

_____

_____

_____

_____

Now that you have your plan, put it into play! I want you to practice this treatment strategy for at least 2 weeks. Once you've done this for 2 weeks, answer the following questions again:

1. Do you find yourself having more difficulties in your significant relationships?

Yes   No

2. Do you feel more irritable or feel as though you have less patience throughout the day?

Yes   No

3. When engaging in enjoyable activities, do you feel like the activity provides less joy than it used too?

Yes   No

4. Are you drinking more alcohol, smoking more, or using prescription medications more frequently to help manage your stress?

Yes   No

5. Do you eat more than you used to or less than you used to?

Yes   No

6. Are you struggling to fall asleep at night? Or do you find yourself consistently waking in the middle of the night?

Yes   No

7. Do you feel lonely or feel as though you have no one you can count on?

Yes   No

8. Do you find yourself feeling frequently anxious?

Yes   No

9. Do you feel like your thoughts are racing or that you can't get negative thoughts out of your head?

Yes   No

Compare your answers to the first time you took this questionnaire. How do they compare? If you find that you are endorsing less of these questions and are starting to feel a little better, that's great! It means your treatment strategy is working. If not, try a new strategy and repeat this *Respond* exercise again. Keep trying different treatment strategies until you find something that is helping you manage your parental burnout.

[1] The questions in this exercise are an adaptation of the "Signs and Symptoms of Parental Burnout" list developed by Michael Hollander in his book *Helping Teens Who Cut: Understanding and Ending Self-Injury*.

[2] In *AoP*, more detail was given to this section, providing descriptions of each suggestion and more in-depth explanations.

[3] Consider re-reading Chapter 12 of *AoP* to gain a fuller understanding of the suggestions being provided here.

[4] If you need some ideas, check out my list of 50 different self-care activities in Appendix B of this book.

13

Becoming a Wholistic Parent

It has been a long journey, but hopefully it has been informative, inspiring, and healing. Parenting is hard work, and so often we find ourselves guessing at how to go about doing it! We want to be the best parent we can be, and we want to raise children that are happy, healthy, and productive members of society one day. In short, we want them to be SUCCESSFUL in all areas of their lives. But that journey of raising successful children starts with us.

So many of us were raised with less than ideal circumstances in our own childhood. Perhaps we experienced abandonment by one or both parents, experienced death, hardship, poverty, or abuse. It's hard to know how to raise your own children when you lacked positive life experiences or healthy role models yourself.

Some of us were privileged, being raised in expensive neighborhoods, living in fancy homes, and going to the best schools. Often, however, high socioeconomic statuses don't shield us from all the ugliness the world can offer. You, too, may have experienced abuse at the hands of others you thought were there to protect you, experienced a traumatic event, experienced the loss of something beloved, or were abandoned by those you relied on most. Indeed, riches often do not save us from horror of the world.

Regardless of your circumstances, regardless of your experiences, and regardless of your own upbringing, you found yourself drawn to this book because you wanted to learn a better way. You wanted to feel more informed, more capable, and less helpless in the raising of your own children. You wanted to learn the fine art that is parenting and provide your family with a wholistic, systemic approach.

13.1 Review

Over the course of this book, we have slowly peeled back the multiple layers of the "parenting onion." Looking at each layer, we developed a fuller understanding that all the components to parenting must be considered individually but executed as a whole. Focusing solely on one part of parenting isn't effective. You must look at all the pieces at once to truly understand how each part intertwines and works with the other. In doing so, you develop a more wholistic approach to parenting.

Here's a breakdown of our journey together in each chapter:

1. We looked at a bird's-eye-view to parenting and developed a general understanding of the concept of *Wholistic Parenting*.

2. You were exposed to my parenting philosophy as a framework for parenting. It was provided to you as an example of what your own parenting philosophy might look like (and, of course, you are welcome to adopt mine).

3. Next, we scratched the surface of a huge topic: the Parent-Child relationship. We reviewed different attachment styles, how they form, and how you can begin to develop a healthy

attachment with your child no matter how old they currently are.

4. You took a hard look at yourself and examined who you currently are as a parent. You learned about the 4 parenting styles and took time to recognize where you currently lie on this continuum. We reviewed the 6 items that affect your parenting and looked at *goodness of fit* with your child.

5. In this section, we dug deeper into the Parent-Child relationship, recognizing how important it really is in happy, healthy, and united families. We touched on the concept of the *Emotional Piggy Bank* and investigated 3 ways you could begin enriching your relationship with your child. Then, we took a brief look at how you can begin repairing a damaged Parent-Child relationship.

6. You received a quick rundown of child development through the different developmental stages: infancy, early childhood, middle childhood, and adolescence.

7. This is where we *really* rolled up our sleeves and began digging deeper into the psychology of it all. In this section, we looked at emotions in children and how emotions affect behavior.

8. After learning about emotions, you were ready to understand the concept of *emotion regulation*. This chapter was a mammoth, touching on the roots of emotion regulation, why some individuals have poor emotion regulation, the *Fight or Flight Response*, and the "how-to's" of coping skills.

9. Your next step was learning about a wholistic approach to discipline. I provided you with a new definition of what discipline is, and you obtained a more wholistic view of how effective discipline works. You learned about structure and routine, rules and limits, and rewards and consequences. I also helped you to understand the subtle differences between bribing versus rewarding and consequences versus punishment.

We broke down the 3 parts to parental consistency, learned 8 tips to effective communication with your kids, reviewed 4 tips for effective *praise*, and investigated the structure of disciplinary sessions.

10. In this section, we defined the individuals who should be considered as *co-parents*, lamented over the difficulties that co-parenting can bring, and discussed how to prevent co-parenting disasters.

11. We reviewed your marriage and how children can unintentionally cause dissention in your romantic relationships. Then, we looked at 4 tips to keeping your marriage happy and healthy while raising kids.

12. Our last stop was a discussion of parental burnout, a very real, negative side-effect to parenting. We not only reviewed how parental burnout can happen but looked at how you can treat AND prevent parental burnout!

Hopefully, you can now see how each part interweaves with the other and needs to be considered and executed as a whole (i.e. *Wholistic* Parenting!).

At the beginning of this book, I informed you that you wouldn't walk away with specific parenting techniques for discipline and such. Although I provided many tips (and *yes*, I couldn't help but provide *some* parenting interventions), my main goal was for you to have a deeper, more foundational understanding of parenting.

In the beginning, I likened parenting to cooking. I explained how, being given a recipe for any dish does not make you a chef (or even a good cook!). In order to truly become a chef, you must understand the mechanics and science of cooking. You must understand the *art* of being a chef. In a similar way, teaching you parenting interventions and/or techniques is like giving you a recipe. It's only good for that one thing. It doesn't make you a better parent at your core, it doesn't help you really understand what is going on with your child, and it certainly doesn't help you understand how to adapt "the recipe" when something isn't working.

That's why you must learn the **gestalt** of it all. You must learn how each part works and how each part connects to the other, creating a fabulous system that moves together as a unit (e.g. the **family system**). That was the goal of this book, to help you see that bigger, bird's-eye-view, to help you adopt a wholistic parenting approach to your own family, and to help you understand the fine art that is parenting. I hope that you got that from this book, even if only a little bit. Because even a little movement in the direction of becoming a more wholistic parent will do wonders in helping you achieve a happier, more loving, and more united family in the long run. That is what I want for you.

13.2 One Small Step

It has been a long journey without a doubt, and hopefully a productive one for you. And after a long journey, we find ourselves always asking the following question:

What do I do now?

The answer is a simple one: you take one small step. Every journey begins with one small step, one small movement in the direction you hope to go. Wholistic Parenting can be incredibly overwhelming... there's just so much to consider at any given time. I've been teaching Wholistic Parenting for years, and *I* even felt overwhelmed when I was trying to write this book. It's ok to feel this way, but that's why you need to start with just one small step.

Throughout the book, I made suggestions of things that you could begin applying to your parenting today, but to try and apply them all at once can overwhelm you. This, in turn, will increase the likelihood that you won't follow through with it and eventually fail. None of us want that.

You've helped yourself become more successful by purchasing this companion workbook, designed with practical exercises to help build your parenting skills. By completing the exercises in this book, you have taken some monumental steps in becoming the best parent you can be while adopting a more wholistic approach to your parenting. Remember, the key to changing behavior and developing new habits is to break the journey down into manageable, baby steps, and the workbook has helped you achieve this.

Continue to take small steps each day. Pick one thing that you want to do differently and start doing that every single day. If you need someone to help keep you accountable, ask a friend or your co-parent to help you out. Don't be overwhelmed by it all; just pick one small step and take it! Remember, this isn't a race, and you aren't competing with anyone. This is a journey of self-growth. You are on the journey of evolving into the best version of your parenting-self, so enjoy it!

13.3 Final Thoughts

I truly love helping people; it's why I became a marriage and family therapist. But parenting is my passion, and that's why it became my specialty. I look forward to writing more books that help parents adopt a wholistic parenting approach, and I plan to continue the *Art of Parenting* series with more specific topics, such as parenting through divorce, parenting teens, and so on. As such, I would love to hear from you!

If you have a topic that you would like me to write about, you can always visit my website at kcdreisbach.com and send me a message with your suggestions. Once you are on the website, you can check out the various parenting articles I've written, covering topics such as parenting children with ADHD, Postpartum Depression, and more, available for you to access at no cost. You can also sign up for my monthly newsletter so that you know when the next book in the series comes out.

***

It has been a great pleasure guiding you in this journey. Once again, I hope you find yourself motivated in becoming the best parent that you can be! You deserve to have a happy, loving life and parenting should be something that adds to that life in a positive way. It shouldn't be a heartache. Hopefully this book has given you the roadmap to that life.

Happy Parenting!

Glossary

Ambivalent/Resistant Attachment- A pattern in which an infant shows distress before a caregiver leaves them, is significantly upset while the caregiver is absent, and then wants and resists contact with their caregiver when the caregiver returns
(Paplia and Feldman 214)

Attachment- A mutual, long-standing bond between two people (particularly between a caregiver and infant) that defines the quality of the relationship (Paplia and Feldman 213)

Authoritarian Parenting Style- A parenting style that is primarily characterized around control and obedience (Paplia and Feldman 301)

Authoritative Parenting Style- A parenting style that honors a child's individuality but balances it with social constraints. Good behavior is demanded with consistent firm standards, but balanced with love and acceptance (Paplia and Feldman 301)

Avoidant Attachment- A pattern of behavior where an infant rarely cries or fusses when they are separated from a caregiver, and then avoids contact or interaction with this caregiver when he/she returns to the infant (Paplia and Feldman 214)

Behavioral Activation- A therapeutic intervention that involve getting the client more engaged and active with pleasurable activities that have the potential to improve the individual's mood (Hindman, *Behavioral Activation*)

Big Five Factors of Personality- The 5 dimensions that many psychologists have determined personality is comprised of: openness, emotional stability, extraversion, agreeableness, and conscientiousness

Co-Parent- Those individuals who are responsible for watching your children a significant amount of the time

Conscientious Parenting- Parenting when you are in control of your emotions. Your words and actions are thought out carefully, and your interactions with your child have purpose and meaning to them.

Coping Skills- Different actions an individual can take in order to help them manage difficult emotions such as anger, anxiety, or sadness

Development- A pattern of biological, cognitive, and socioemotional processes that begins when a person is conceived and spans throughout the years of his/her life (Santrock 28)

Difficult Child- A temperament style where the child has intense emotional reactions, often negative and aggressive in nature. Children with this temperament lack self-control and are slow to accept new experiences (Santrock 136)

Discipline- Techniques used to shape a child's character and behavior. These techniques teach self-control and encourage acceptable behavior (Paplia and Feldman 298)

Disciplinary Session- When and how you engage in disciplining your child

Disorganized/Disoriented Attachment- A behavioral pattern in which an infant (after being left alone by the caregiver) will show different, contradictory behaviors when the caregiver returns (Paplia and Feldman 214)

Easy Child- A temperament style where the child has mild reactions, often positive and well-humored in nature. Children with this temperament are often in a good mood, quickly adapt to new experiences, and easily settle into regular routines (Santrock 136)

Emotion Regulation- The process by which a person manages their emotions

Emotional Piggy Bank- Analogy used to explain how relationships work

Ethnic Culture- A family's connection to their ethnicity and the related characteristics, spiritual beliefs, language, customs, and cultural heritage that the family follows and adheres too

External Coping Skills- Coping skills that exist outside of yourself or require a physical object to work, such as a stress ball

Familial Environment- This consists of your home and the multiple parts that go with it, such as each family member.

Familial Stress- All of the stressful events, interactions, and experiences that cause you stress within your family and household

Family Narrative- The story of your family, as told by any given person in your family.

Family System- A conceptual understanding of the family unit in which the family is a connected system comprised of multiple individual parts that function together (Nichols 461)

Fight or Flight Response- "Response to an acute threat to survival that is marked by physical changes, including nervous and endocrine changes, that prepare a human or an animal to react or to retreat" (Editors of Encyclopaedia Britannica). See also *Stress Response.*

Frustration Tolerance- This is the ability to adapt and overcome challenges, obstacles, and other stressors (Esposito, *Frazzled*)

Gestalt- "A configuration or pattern of elements so unified as a whole that its properties cannot be derived from a simple summation of its parts" ("Gestalt," def. 1)

Goodness of Fit- When the parental and environmental demands of a child's environment matches the child's temperament and ability to meet those demands (Paplia and Feldman 211)

Individuation- The normal process by which an individual struggles for autonomy and personal identity separate from other people (Paplia and Feldman 455)

Indulgent Parenting Style- A style of parenting that allows children to govern their own activities as much as possible. Discipline is infrequent, and parents are typically warm, noncontrolling, and indulgent (Santrock 77). See also *Permissive Parenting Style.*

Internal Coping Skills- Coping skills that utilize nothing but yourself, such as Deep Breathing

Layering Coping Skills- The act of using one skill, then the next, over and over again until you have regained control of your emotions

Love Maps- John Gottman's term for the all the information you have stored in your brain about your partner and their life (Gottman and Silver 48)

Microcosm- "A small, representative system having analogies to a larger system in constitution, configuration, or development" (The American Heritage Dictionary 535)

Modeling- The act of showing your children how to act and react in any given situation by a role model and acting in the desired way yourself

Natural Anxiety- The normal, healthy level of anxiety existent in all people

Nature vs Nurture- *Nature* refers to the biological, genetic make-up of a person, whereas *nurture* refers to the interactions the person had with their parents as they grew up

Neglectful Parenting Style- A style characterized by a lack of involvement. These parents rarely spend quality time with their children, know little about their children, and they fail to provide structure and/or healthy boundaries (Santrock 77)

Parent-Child Relational Triangle- When a child has been brought into the relational problems between parents. *Example: A father complains to a child about the mother's actions.*

Parent-Child Relationship- The essential bond and connection you have with your child

Parental Consistency- Parenting in the same way between all children in the home, from day to day, and in a similar way to your co-parent

Parental Sabotage- When someone undermines your parenting

Permissive Parenting Style- A parenting style that in which children govern most of their own activities. Power lies primarily with the children, and discipline is seldom used. Parents who utilize this style are often warm in nature, indulgent, demand little (if anything) from their children, and are noncontrolling (Paplia and Feldman 301). See also *Indulgent Parenting Style.*

Personality- A mixture of emotions, thoughts, temperament, and behaviors that remain consistent over time. This mixture is what makes each person unique in who they are and how they interact with the world (Paplia and Feldman 204)

Quality Time- Spending time engaging in an activity that the other person enjoys

Reactive Parenting- Whenever you are parenting from an emotional state (namely when you are angry)

Relaxation Response- A biological response governed by the Parasympathetic branch of the Autonomic Nervous System

Secure Attachment- A pattern in which an infant is able to to find comfort from their caregiver easily and effectively in the face of a stressful situation (Paplia and Feldman 214)

Slow-to-Warm-Up Child- A temperament style in which the child displays low emotional intensity. These children struggle to adapt, are somewhat negative, and display low levels of activity (Santrock 136)

Social Culture- The related characteristics, spiritual beliefs, languages, customs, and cultural heritage of the society in which a family lives

Social Environment- This is the outside world that your family lives in. It consists of your neighborhood, social networks, country, and current events.

Social Influence- This consists of the people that might influence you or your child

Stress Response- A biological response governed by the Sympathetic branch of the Autonomic Nervous System. See also *Fight or Flight Response*

Tantrum (Temper Tantrum)- "A fit of bad temper" (The American Heritage Dictionary 837)

Temperament- A person's style of managing life situations (Paplia and Feldman 209)

Triangulation- The process of pulling a third person into a relational conflict to help ease tension rather than managing the conflict in the original pair (Gilbert 74)

Wholistic- "The philosophy that all parts of a thing are interconnected. In medicine, wholistic treatment is the treatment of a person as a whole, mind, body and social factors" (The Grammarist Team, *Wholistic and holistic*)

Wholistic Discipline- A component to the Wholistic Parenting approach; consists of punishment, rewards, praise, structure, consistency, healthy boundaries, love and affection, rules and limits

Wholistic Parenting- Considering the mind, body, and social environment of your family and shaping your parenting to those factors

Appendix A

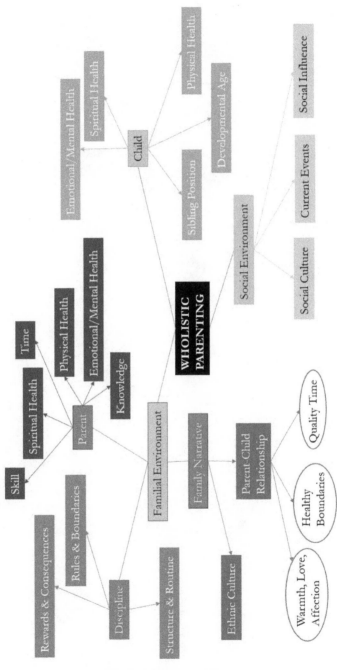

Wholistic Parenting Map
K.C. Dreisbach, LMFT

Appendix B

Appendix B

Enjoy this list of 50 different ideas for engaging in self-care and stress relief. There are more choices than just the ones listed, but I wanted to show you ideas that shouldn't cost you any extra money out of your pocket. Try to apply a few ideas throughout the week. For simpler ideas, such as journaling, try to apply it daily for optimum stress relief.

1. Journaling
2. Keeping a gratitude journal
3. Painting
4. Sculpting
5. Dancing
6. Working out at the gym
7. Enjoying a special treat or drink
8. Going for a walk
9. Going for a hike
10. Going for a bike ride
11. Swimming
12. Going for a drive in the car
13. 10 minutes of quiet time or napping
14. Practicing Deep Breathing/Belly Breathing
15. Progressive Muscle Relaxation
16. Taking a shower
17. Taking a bubble bath
18. Reading a book
19. Reading a magazine
20. Doing a puzzle
21. Doing a logic puzzle or word search
22. Playing a video game

23. 10 minutes surfing the web
24. Completing Grounding exercises
25. Meditating
26. Stretching exercises
27. Practicing mindfulness
28. Giving yourself a manicure or pedicure
29. Practicing yoga poses
30. Going to sleep 10 minutes early
31. Sleeping in by 10 minutes
32. Watch a movie
33. Watch an episode of your favorite TV show
34. Call a friend
35. Listen to music
36. Play an instrument
37. Sing
38. Practicing positive affirmations
39. Practice self-forgiveness
40. Having a picnic
41. Listen to an audiobook during long commutes
42. If you have a pet, taking 5-10 minutes to play with it
43. Going for a run
44. Write poetry
45. Read poetry
46. Bake or cook something enjoyable
47. Garden
48. Do photography
49. Take 5-10 minutes to look at photobooks of pleasant memories
50. Read motivational essays or books

References

Amsel, Beverly. *Individuation.* 6 September 2019. 2 August 2020. www.goodther-apy.org/learn-about-therapy/issues/individuation.

"Bribe, *Verb.*" *Lexico Dictionary,* Oxford University Press; Dictionary.com. 2020. www.lexico.com/en/definition/bribe.

Chess, S and A Thomas. "Temperamental Individuality from Childhood to Adolescence." *Journal of Child Psychiatry* 16 (1977): 218-226.

"Consequence, *Noun 1.*" *Lexico Dictionary,* Oxford University Press; Dictionay.com. 2020. www.lexico.com/definition/consequence.

DeRaad, B. "The trait-coverage of emotional intelligence." *Personality & Individual Differences* 2005: 673-687.

The American Heritage Dictionary. New York: Houghton Mifflin Company, 2001.

Dreisbach, K.C. *Trials of the Working Parent: A busy mom's guide to kids, work & loving yourself.* Covina: K.C. Dreisbach, LMFT, 2019.

Editors of Encyclopaedia Brtannica. "Fight-or-flight response." *Britannica.* Encyclopaedia Britannica, Inc. 12 August 2019, www.britannica.com/science/fight-or-flight-response.

Esposito, Linda. *Frazzled: High anxiety and low frustration tolerance.* 28 November 2017. www.psychologytoday.com/us/blog/anxiety-zen/201711/frazzled-high-anxiety-and-low-frustration-tolerance.

Gilbert, Roberta M. *Extraordinary Relationships: A New Way of Thinking about Human Interactions.* New York: John Wiley & Sons, Inc, 1992.

Good Therapy. *Triangulation.* 1 August 2016. 2 August 2020. www.goodther-apy.org/blog/psychpedia/triangulation.

Gottman, John and Nan Silver. *The Seven Principles for Making Marriage Work.* New York: Three Rivers Press, 1999.

Hindman, Robert. *Behavioral Activation Tip.* 21 February 2018. beckinstitute.org/be-havioral-activation-tip/.

Lee, K., M.C. Ashton and K-H Shin. "Personality Correlates of Workplace Anti-Social Behavior." *Applied Psychology: An International Review* n.d.: 81-97.

Lieberman, Alicia F. *The Emotional Life of the Toddler.* New York: Simon & Schuster, 2018.

Mayo Clinic. *Healthy Lifestyle: Stress Management.* 2020. 2 August 2020. www.mayoclinic.org/healthy-lifestyle/stress-management/in-depth/stress/art-20046037.

McCrae, R.R. and P.T. Costa. *Personality in Adulthood.* 2nd. New York: Guilford, 2003.

Miller-Karas, Elaine and Laurie Leitch. *Trauma Resiliency Model Workbook.* 2013.

Nichols, Michael P. *Family Therapy: Concepts and Methods.* Boston: Allyn & Bacon, 2010.

Paplia, Diane E and Ruth Duskin Feldman. *A Child's World: Infancy through Adolescence.* New York: McGraw-Hill, 2011.

"Philosophy, *2.b*" *Oxford American Dictionary and Thesaurus*, Oxford University Press, 2003, p.1121.

"Punishment, *Noun 1.*" *Lexico Dictionary*, Oxford University Press; Disctionary.com. 2020. www.lexico.com/definition/punishment.

"Reward, *Noun 1.*" *Lexico Dictionary*, Oxford University Press; Disctionary.com. 2020. www.lexico.com/definition/reward.

Santrock, John W. *Educational Psychology.* 3rd. McGraw-Hill Companies, Inc, 2008.

Selva, Joaquin. *Behavioural Activation: Behavioural Therapy for Depression Treatment.* 8 July 2020. 2 August 2020. positivepsychology.com/behavioural-activation-therapy-treating-depression/.

Grammarist. *Wholistis and holistic.* 24 April 2020. grammarist.com/spelling/wholistic-and-holistic/.

More by K.C. Dreisbach

MORE BY K.C. DREISBACH

Trials of the Working Parent: A Busy Mom's Guide to Kids, Work & Loving Yourself

The Art of Parenting: How to Parent from Infancy to Adulthood

ABOUT THE AUTHOR

Krystal Dreisbach is a licensed marriage and family therapist, international author, and parenting expert. Her specialties include trauma, depression, anxiety, and parenting. She is the author of several books and in the founder of The Wholistic Family Blog. She completed her graduate training at Loma Linda University School of Behavioral Health where she earned her master's of science in Marital & Family Therapy.

Ms. Dreisbach resides in the greater Los Angeles area, where she owns a private practice, providing mental health services and clinical supervision. She is a member of the California Association for Marriage and Family Therapist, and a former member of the American Association for Marriage and Family Therapists. She offers psychotherapy and parenting services to clients in the greater Los Angeles, CA area, and throughout the state of California through her telehealth private practice.

CPSIA information can be obtained
at www.ICGtesting.com
Printed in the USA
LVHW031058130421
684340LV00008B/151